THE COMPLETE GUIDE TO
Animals

A New Burlington Book
Conceived, edited, and designed by Marshall Editions
The Old Brewery, 6 Blundell Street, London N7 9BH, UK
www.quarto.com

Publisher: Richard Green
Commissioning editor: Claudia Martin
Art director: Ivo Marloh
Design and editorial: Tall Tree
Production: Nikki Ingram
Consultant: Mandy Holloway

ISBN 10: 1–84566–094–3
ISBN 13: 978–1–84566–094–9

Originated in Hong Kong by Modern Age
Printed and bound in China by
SNP Leefung Printers Limited

10 9 8 7 6 5 4 3 2 1

THE COMPLETE GUIDE TO
Animals

Jinny Johnson
General consultant: Professor Philip Whitfield

Contents

Introduction

The staggering array of animals that inhabit all corners of the Earth can be divided into two main groups: vertebrates (animals with backbones) and invertebrates (animals without backbones). Mammals, birds, reptiles, amphibians, and fish all have backbones, while insects, spiders, and mollusks do not.

Habitats around the world

Animals live everywhere on Earth—in every kind of terrain and every kind of climate. An animal's natural home or environment is called its habitat. Most animals are only adapted to live in only one or two habitats. A barracuda, for example, is a saltwater fish and could not live in a freshwater lake; a seal could not live in a desert; and a rattlesnake could not live for very long in the Arctic. Some animals migrate in the spring and again in the fall to find warmer habitats with an abundance of food. The varying climates around the world create vastly different climate and plant life zones, from hot, dry deserts and hot, wet rain forests to freezing polar deserts, deep oceans, open grasslands, and freshwater lakes and rivers. The animals that live in these different environments have evolved a staggeringly diverse range of different ways to live, feed, and breed.

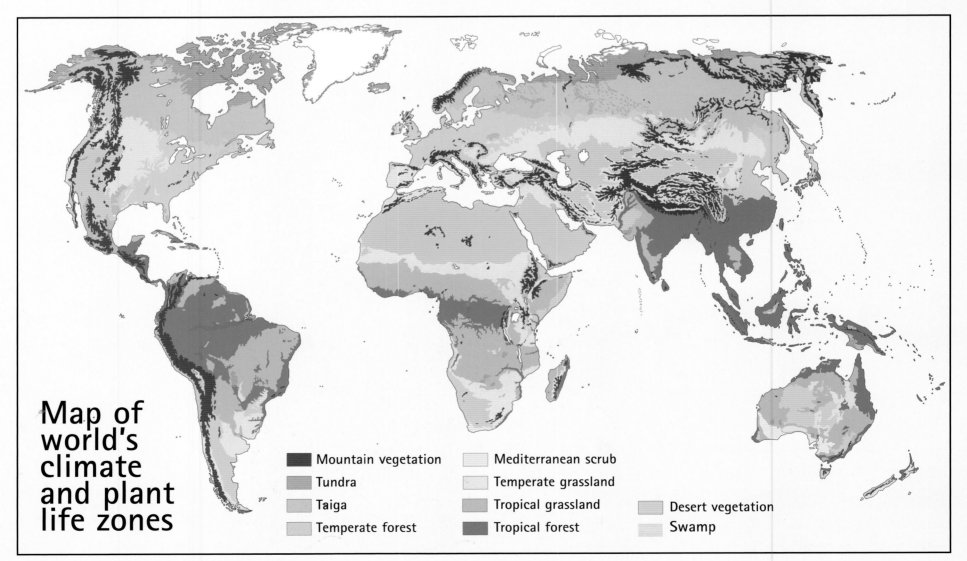

Map of world's climate and plant life zones

Mountain vegetation	Mediterranean scrub
Tundra	Temperate grassland
Taiga	Tropical grassland
Temperate forest	Tropical forest

Desert vegetation
Swamp

How to use this book

The animals in these pages are arranged in chapters corresponding to the main animal groups: mammals, reptiles, birds, fish, and so on. Families or related species are grouped on each double-page spread. Individual entries are headed by the most generally accepted version of the animal's common name.

African elephant

Scale The silhouettes compare the size of the animal with the size of an average adult human body, hand, or head and shoulders.

Latin name Either the specific species name or the family name is given.

Size The approximate size of the whole animal, or of a specific part of the animal, is given.

Habitat and **Distribution** Habitat information tells you what kind of environment the animal lives in. The distribution data and map tell you which parts of the world it lives in.

Map The red areas indicate the regions that the species inhabits.

Latin name	*Loxodonta africana*
Size	Body length: up to 25 ft (7.5 m)
Habitat	Forest, savanna
Distribution	Sub-Saharan Africa

African elephant

The African elephant has larger ears and tusks than the Asian species and two fingerlike extensions at the end of its trunk. They are social animals, and live in troops centered around several females and their young of various ages. As they mature, young males separate to form separate all-male troops.

Ocean zones

The ocean can be divided into zones. Most plants and animals live in the warm, light zone at the top, called the euphotic or sunlit zone. Below this, the dysphotic or twilight zone is too murky for plants to grow; animals that live here include lantern fish and giant squid. No light reaches the aphotic or midnight zone. Only strange creatures such as the angler fish and gulper eel live here. At the bottom, the sea bed is home to sea cucumbers and brittle stars.

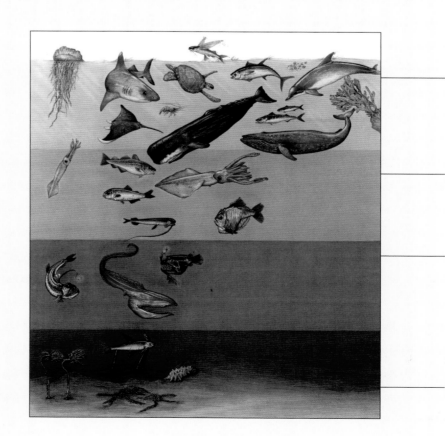

Euphotic or sunlit zone is about 0–600 ft (0–200 m) deep

Dysphotic or twilight zone is about 600–3,300 ft (200–1,000 m) deep

Aphotic or midnight zone extends to the sea bed. It includes most of the oceans' water and is more than 36,000 ft (11,000 m) deep in places

Sea bed or benthic zone

What is an animal?

There are many kinds of living things, and we divide them into five groups called kingdoms. Fungi, bacteria, algae, and the tiny invisible organisms in every drop of water are all alive and must reproduce and obtain food, just like animals and plants. Some make their own food, while others consume other organisms. Animals are much more developed than other living things.

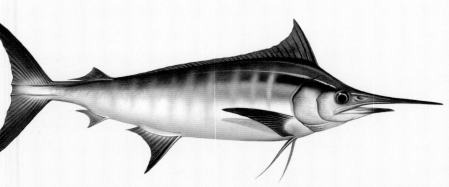

The **blue marlin** is a type of fish. Like all fish, the marlin is adapted to take oxygen from water, rather than air.

With its feathery tentacles, a **sea anemone** might look more like a plant, but it is an animal that lives, breathes, and feeds.

KINGDOM MONERA	KINGDOM PROTISTA	KINGDOM FUNGI	KINGDOM PLANTAE	KINGDOM ANIMALIA
Includes bacteria, blue-green algae	Includes amoeba, some algae	Includes molds, mushrooms, yeasts	All plants, including mosses and ferns	All animals, from sponges to apes
MAIN CHARACTERISTICS	**MAIN CHARACTERISTICS**	**MAIN CHARACTERISTICS**	**MAIN CHARACTERISTICS**	**MAIN CHARACTERISTICS**
Organization Monocellular (made up of only one cell)	**Organization** Monocellular (made up of only one cell)	**Organization** Multicellular (made up of many cells)	**Organization** Multicellular (made up of many cells)	**Organization** Multicellular (made up of many cells)
Cell structure Cell does not have a true nucleus	**Cell structure** Cell has a nucleus	**Cell structure** Cells have nuclei	**Cell structure** Cells have nuclei	**Cell structure** Cells have nuclei
Movement Some can move by means of a tail-like flagellum.	**Movement** Some protista can move, others cannot	**Movement** Cannot move around	**Movement** Cannot move around	**Movement** Most can move at some stage of the life cycle
Feeding Some make their own food. Others break down other living organisms.	**Feeding** Some can make their own food. Others feed on other organisms.	**Feeding** Most feed on dead or decaying organisms. They cannot make their own food.	**Feeding** Make their own food from sunlight, carbon dioxide, and water	**Feeding** Cannot make their own food, but feed on plants and/or other animals

A **tiger salamander** is an amphibian—a type of animal that can live in water and on land.

Animals are divided into two main groups: vertebrates (animals with backbones) and invertebrates (animals without backbones). The vertebrate group includes fish, amphibians, reptiles, birds, and mammals. The invertebrates include creatures such as worms, sponges, mollusks, and insects. You might be surprised to see that all of the creatures on these pages are animals.

Birds, like this **hummingbird**, are the only animals with feathers, which keep them warm and allow them to fly.

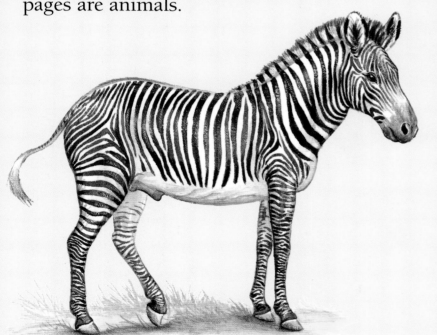

The **zebra** is a mammal—a warm-blooded, hairy animal. Zebras are plant eaters, but some mammals feed on other animals.

Signs of life

There are seven main "signs of life" that distinguish living things from non-living objects, and animals have all seven.

Animals:
- **Breathe** in order to get oxygen into the body to help fuel the body's processes
- **Reproduce**, most of them sexually, although a few simple animals reproduce by making identical "copies" of themselves; in sexual reproduction, a male and female sex cell join together to make a new individual
- **Move around**, in order to find food, mates, or escape from danger; even some of those that appear not to move, such as barnacles, have young that swim freely before settling on a rock
- **Feed** on other organisms (plants or animals) in order to make energy for the body; animals also need to drink water
- **Sense** the world around them by sight, smell, touch, hearing, and/or taste
- **Grow**, both to reach full size and to repair damage in the body
- **Excrete**, or remove waste products from the body—animals breathe out carbon dioxide and get rid of other waste in the form of urine and faeces.

A **butterfly** is a kind of insect, the most common type of animal on Earth.

Snakes are reptiles, cold-blooded animals that rely on the sun for warmth.

Animal classification

Many more than a million species of animal have already been described and scientists estimate that there may be tens of millions more yet to be discovered. Scientists classify the animal kingdom into different groups. A brown bear, for instance, is a *species* of bear—a species is a group of very similar organisms that can breed together. Bears belong to the bear *family*, which belongs the *order* of carnivores, which is in the *class* of mammals, which is part of the *phylum* called *chordates* (chordates are animals with backbones). The chart below shows the main animal groups.

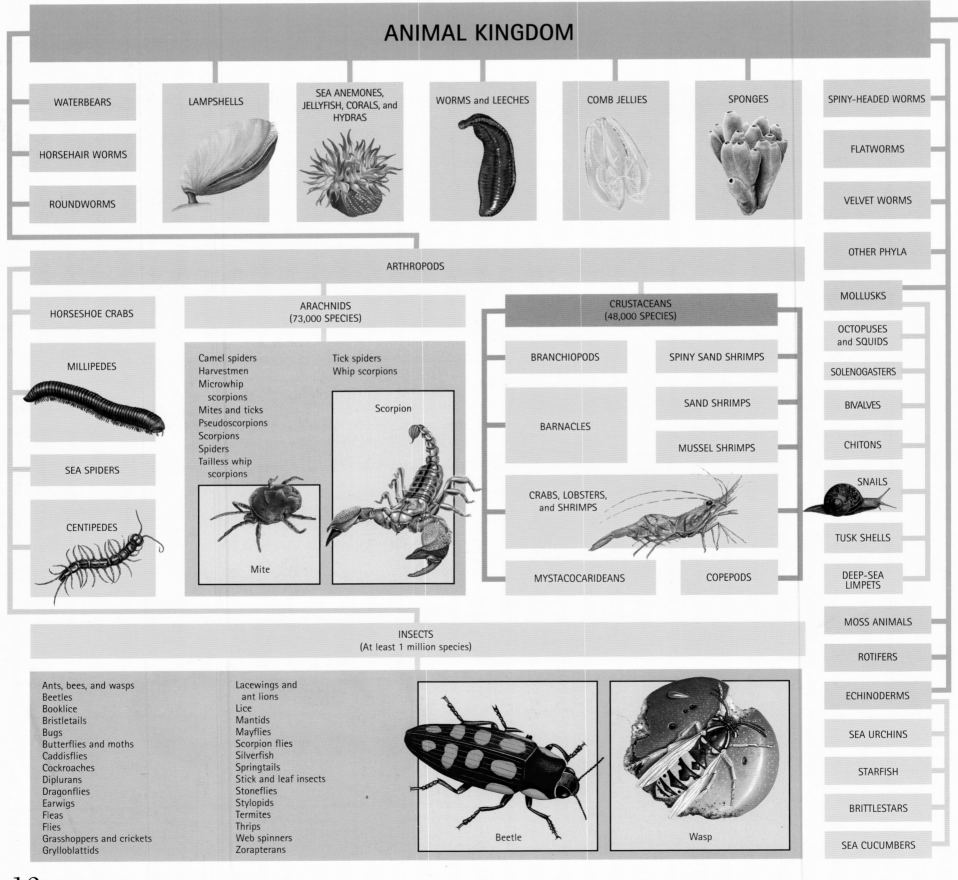

ANIMAL KINGDOM

WATERBEARS

HORSEHAIR WORMS

ROUNDWORMS

LAMPSHELLS

SEA ANEMONES, JELLYFISH, CORALS, and HYDRAS

WORMS and LEECHES

COMB JELLIES

SPONGES

SPINY-HEADED WORMS

FLATWORMS

VELVET WORMS

OTHER PHYLA

MOLLUSKS

OCTOPUSES and SQUIDS

SOLENOGASTERS

BIVALVES

CHITONS

SNAILS

TUSK SHELLS

DEEP-SEA LIMPETS

MOSS ANIMALS

ROTIFERS

ECHINODERMS

SEA URCHINS

STARFISH

BRITTLESTARS

SEA CUCUMBERS

ARTHROPODS

HORSESHOE CRABS

MILLIPEDES

SEA SPIDERS

CENTIPEDES

ARACHNIDS (73,000 SPECIES)

Camel spiders
Harvestmen
Microwhip scorpions
Mites and ticks
Pseudoscorpions
Scorpions
Spiders
Tailless whip scorpions

Tick spiders
Whip scorpions

Scorpion

Mite

CRUSTACEANS (48,000 SPECIES)

BRANCHIOPODS

BARNACLES

CRABS, LOBSTERS, and SHRIMPS

MYSTACOCARIDEANS

SPINY SAND SHRIMPS

SAND SHRIMPS

MUSSEL SHRIMPS

COPEPODS

INSECTS (At least 1 million species)

Ants, bees, and wasps
Beetles
Booklice
Bristletails
Bugs
Butterflies and moths
Caddisflies
Cockroaches
Diplurans
Dragonflies
Earwigs
Fleas
Flies
Grasshoppers and crickets
Grylloblattids

Lacewings and ant lions
Lice
Mantids
Mayflies
Scorpion flies
Silverfish
Springtails
Stick and leaf insects
Stoneflies
Stylopids
Termites
Thrips
Web spinners
Zorapterans

Beetle

Wasp

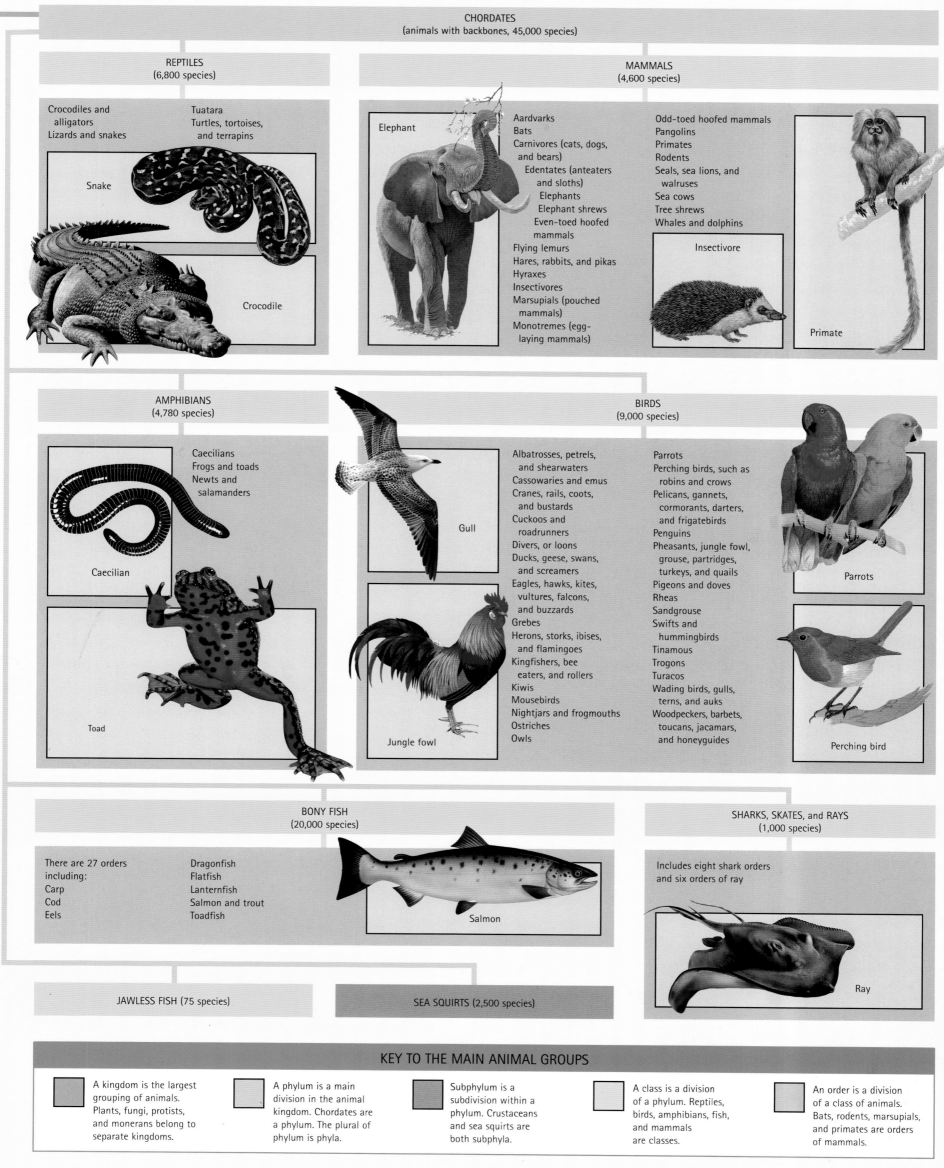

CHORDATES
(animals with backbones, 45,000 species)

REPTILES
(6,800 species)

Crocodiles and
  alligators
Lizards and snakes

Tuatara
Turtles, tortoises,
  and terrapins

Snake

Crocodile

MAMMALS
(4,600 species)

Elephant

Aardvarks
Bats
Carnivores (cats, dogs,
  and bears)
  Edentates (anteaters
    and sloths)
  Elephants
  Elephant shrews
  Even-toed hoofed
    mammals
Flying lemurs
Hares, rabbits, and pikas
Hyraxes
Insectivores
Marsupials (pouched
  mammals)
Monotremes (egg-
  laying mammals)

Odd-toed hoofed mammals
Pangolins
Primates
Rodents
Seals, sea lions, and
  walruses
Sea cows
Tree shrews
Whales and dolphins

Insectivore

Primate

AMPHIBIANS
(4,780 species)

Caecilians
Frogs and toads
Newts and
  salamanders

Caecilian

Toad

BIRDS
(9,000 species)

Gull

Jungle fowl

Albatrosses, petrels,
  and shearwaters
Cassowaries and emus
Cranes, rails, coots,
  and bustards
Cuckoos and
  roadrunners
Divers, or loons
Ducks, geese, swans,
  and screamers
Eagles, hawks, kites,
  vultures, falcons,
  and buzzards
Grebes
Herons, storks, ibises,
  and flamingoes
Kingfishers, bee
  eaters, and rollers
Kiwis
Mousebirds
Nightjars and frogmouths
Ostriches
Owls

Parrots
Perching birds, such as
  robins and crows
Pelicans, gannets,
  cormorants, darters,
  and frigatebirds
Penguins
Pheasants, jungle fowl,
  grouse, partridges,
  turkeys, and quails
Pigeons and doves
Rheas
Sandgrouse
Swifts and
  hummingbirds
Tinamous
Trogons
Turacos
Wading birds, gulls,
  terns, and auks
Woodpeckers, barbets,
  toucans, jacamars,
  and honeyguides

Parrots

Perching bird

BONY FISH
(20,000 species)

There are 27 orders
including:
Carp
Cod
Eels

Dragonfish
Flatfish
Lanternfish
Salmon and trout
Toadfish

Salmon

SHARKS, SKATES, and RAYS
(1,000 species)

Includes eight shark orders
and six orders of ray

Ray

JAWLESS FISH (75 species)

SEA SQUIRTS (2,500 species)

KEY TO THE MAIN ANIMAL GROUPS

A kingdom is the largest
grouping of animals.
Plants, fungi, protists,
and monerans belong to
separate kingdoms.

A phylum is a main
division in the animal
kingdom. Chordates are
a phylum. The plural of
phylum is phyla.

Subphylum is a
subdivision within a
phylum. Crustaceans
and sea squirts are
both subphyla.

A class is a division
of a phylum. Reptiles,
birds, amphibians, fish,
and mammals
are classes.

An order is a division
of a class of animals.
Bats, rodents, marsupials,
and primates are orders
of mammals.

Mammals

Mammals are warm-blooded animals that have lungs for breathing air and a bony frame called a skeleton; they also feed their young on milk. The majority give birth to live young and are covered in hair or fur. Most mammals also have large brains and keen senses.

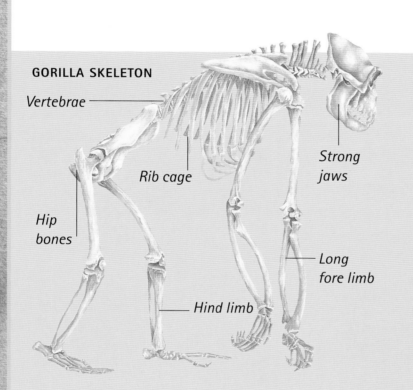

Mammal skeletons

GORILLA SKELETON

Vertebrae

Rib cage

Hip bones

Strong jaws

Long fore limb

Hind limb

A mammal is a vertebrate animal, which means that it has a backbone made up of individual bones called vertebrae. A rib cage surrounds and protects the heart and lungs and a strong, bony skull protects the brain. Hanging from this central section of the skeleton are four limbs. In many mammals, these limbs consist of four legs, or they may be made up of two legs and two arms. In the case of aquatic mammals, the rear limbs have all but disappeared, leaving behind a powerful tail, which these swimming mammals flick to push them through the water.

Hairy mammals

All mammals have hair. Aquatic mammals, such as whales, have little hair on the body because excessive hair would slow the animal down as it swam through the water. Other animals, however, need a lot of hair to keep them warm in cold conditions. Musk oxen, for instance, have a coat with two kinds of hair, one long and one short. These work together to insulate the animals in extremely cold conditions. The hair on a sloth's body grows in the opposite direction to that of other mammals. It points downward when the sloth is hanging in its normal position so that water runs down and off its body.

Two-toed sloth

Marsupials

There are about 280 species of marsupial mammals, including animals such as wombats and koalas as well as kangaroos. Most live in Australasia, but there are more than 70 kinds of opossum in South America and one species, the Virginia opossum, in North America. The word marsupial means "pouched mammal." A marsupial's young are born at a very underdeveloped stage—some are no bigger than a grain of rice, and all are hairless and blind. The babies must make their way to the furry pouch on the underside of the mother's body. Here they can feed on her milk and grow and develop in safety.

Latin name	*Dendrolagus lumholtzi*
Size	Body: 20–32 in (52–80 cm)
Habitat	Rain forest
Distribution	N.E. Queensland

Lumholtz's tree kangaroo

The tree kangaroo spends most of its time high up in the forest trees, where it eats leaves and fruit. It can even sleep up there, crouched on a thick branch. Its numbers are dwindling because logging is causing its rain forest habitat to shrink. Small groups live together and sleep in the same tree. They are not rare but they are very secretive.

Red kangaroo

Red kangaroo

The red kangaroo is the largest marsupial. It usually bounds along on its back legs only, making huge leaps and reaching speeds of up to 35 mph (56 km/h). It lives in Australia's hot deserts and grasslands. The female gives birth to a single baby called a joey, which emerges from her pouch at the age of two months.

Latin name	*Macropus rufus*
Size	Body: 3¼–5¼ ft (1–1.6 m)
Habitat	Grassy, arid plains
Distribution	Central Australia

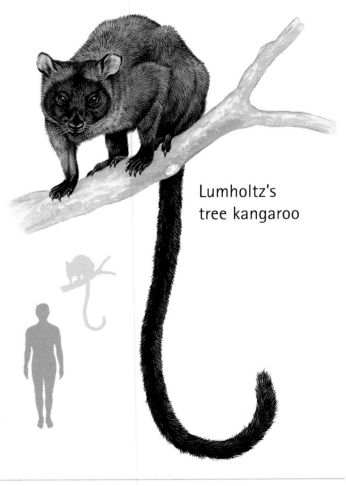

Lumholtz's tree kangaroo

Greater glider possum

Greater glider possum

The greater glider has flaps of skin running between its wrists and ankles. To get from tree to tree in the eucalyptus forests where it lives, it leaps into the air and spreads out its arms and legs. The skin flaps act like a kind of parachute, allowing it to glide to its destination.

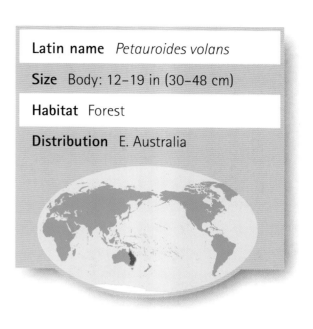

Latin name	*Petauroides volans*
Size	Body: 12–19 in (30–48 cm)
Habitat	Forest
Distribution	E. Australia

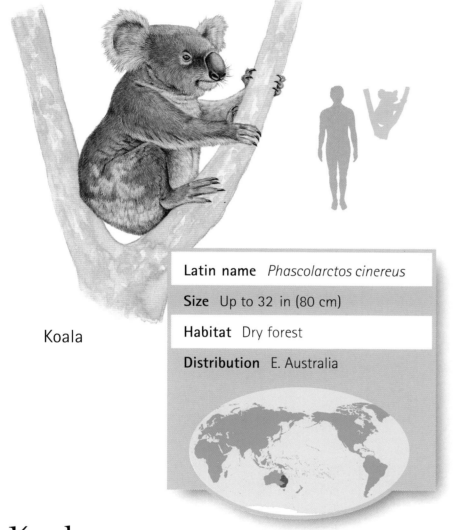

Koala

Latin name	*Phascolarctos cinereus*
Size	Up to 32 in (80 cm)
Habitat	Dry forest
Distribution	E. Australia

Koala

The koala spends up to 18 hours each day asleep. The rest of the time it feeds on the leaves of eucalyptus trees and rarely leaves the trees. It has a long gut, which enables it to digest the tough leaves and deal with the leaves' poisonous chemicals. Special pouches in its cheeks store the leaves until it needs to eat them.

Common wombat

The wombat feeds on grass in forests and scrubland and can go without water for months at a time. In high summer, this burly mammal spends the day in a long, deep burrow, sheltered from the heat. The female gives birth to a single young, which stays in her pouch for three months.

Common wombat

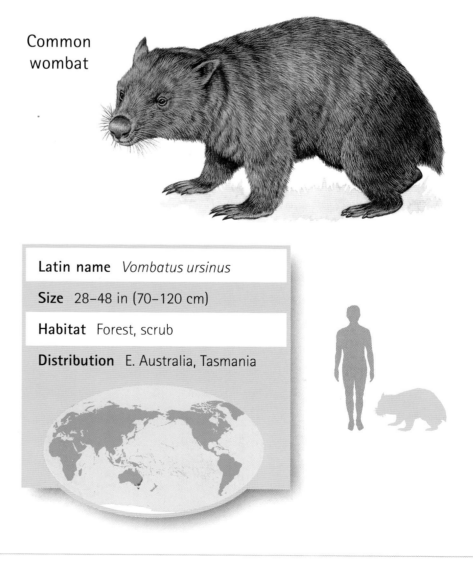

Latin name	*Vombatus ursinus*
Size	28–48 in (70–120 cm)
Habitat	Forest, scrub
Distribution	E. Australia, Tasmania

Virginia opossum

This is the only marsupial native to North America. It often scavenges for food in dumps and garbage bins. To escape a predator, the opossum may "play dead," lying on its side with its tongue hanging out and its eyes shut or staring into space. Thinking it is dead, the predator may become less cautious, giving the opossum a chance to escape.

Latin name	*Didelphis virginiana*
Size	Body: 13–20 in (33–50 cm)
Habitat	Forest, scrubland
Distribution	S.E. Canada to Central America

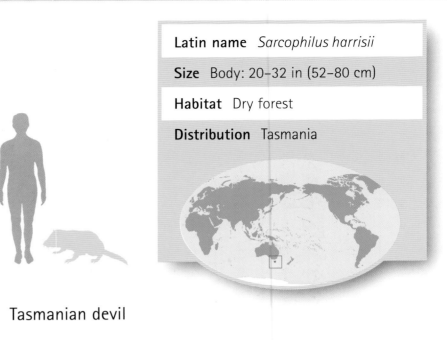

Tasmanian devil

Latin name	*Sarcophilus harrisii*
Size	Body: 20–32 in (52–80 cm)
Habitat	Dry forest
Distribution	Tasmania

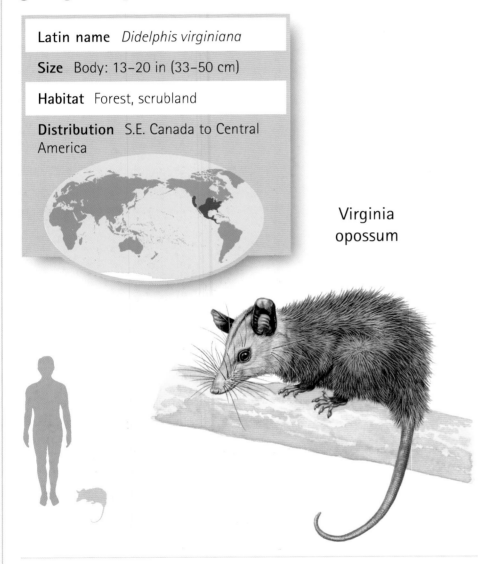

Virginia opossum

Tasmanian devil

This powerfully built marsupial has the reputation of being a vicious killer of sheep and, as a result, great numbers were once hunted by farmers. It is about the size of a small dog and has powerful jaws that enable it to crush the bones of its prey. This stocky marsupial feeds on reptiles, birds, fish, small mammals, and the remains of larger, dead animals.

Short-tailed opossum

Although the short-tailed opossum lives in forested country, it is a poor climber and tends to stay on the forest floor. During the day it shelters in a leafy nest, which it builds in a hollow log or tree trunk. It emerges at night to feed on seeds, shoots, and fruit.

Latin name	*Monodelphis brevicaudata*
Size	Body: 4–5 in (11–14 cm)
Habitat	Forest
Distribution	Venezuela to northern Argentina

Short-tailed opossum

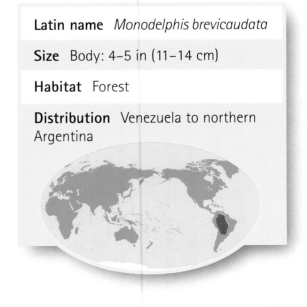

Monotremes

In most mammal species the young grow inside their mother's body. Monotremes are different from any other mammals because, just like reptiles, they lay eggs. However, when the eggs hatch, the young monotremes feed on their mother's milk like other mammal babies. The milk oozes from enlarged skin pores (female monotremes have no nipples). There are only three kinds of monotreme—the platypus, the short-beaked echidna, and the long-beaked echidna. The long-beaked echidna lives in New Guinea. Echidnas are sometimes known as spiny anteaters.

Short-beaked echidna

Duck-billed platypus

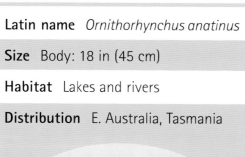

Short-beaked echidna

The short-beaked echidna has a compact, round body that is covered in a spiny coat. When threatened, it either curls into a ball or, if it is on soft soil, it digs straight down so that only its spines are visible. This protects its soft spineless face and underparts. Its tongue is coated with sticky saliva, so that any insect it touches is trapped.

Duck-billed platypus

The platypus a semi-aquatic animal that spends most of the day in a riverside burrow. At dawn and dusk it comes out to feed on the riverbed, using its sensitive bill to probe the mud for insects, worms, grubs, crayfish, and frogs. Its bill is a skin-covered framework of bone. The rear ankles of the male have spurs that are connected to poison glands.

Latin name *Ornithorhynchus anatinus*

Size Body: 18 in (45 cm)

Habitat Lakes and rivers

Distribution E. Australia, Tasmania

Latin name *Tachyglossus aculeatus*

Size Body: 14–20 in (35–50 cm)

Habitat Grassland, forest

Distribution Australia, New Guinea

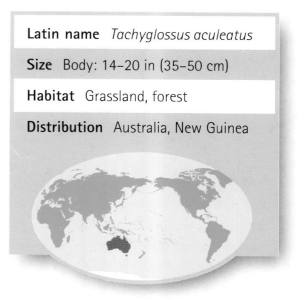

Rabbits, hares, and squirrels

Rabbits, hares, and squirrels all belong to the large group of small to medium-size mammals called rodents. There are at least 2,000 species of rodents, and they are found all over the world in every kind of habitat. Most feed on plants, and they have a pair of sharp incisor teeth in each jaw that allows them to bite through the toughest foods. Pikas, rabbits, and hares are a successful group of plant-eating rodents known as lagomorphs.

Brown hare

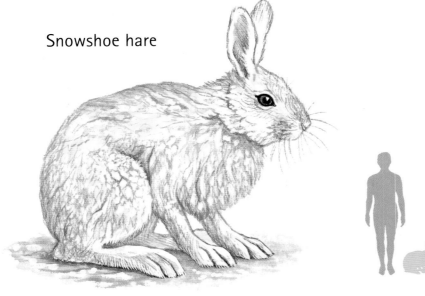

Snowshoe hare

Brown hare

A fast-running hare, with long hind limbs, the brown, or European hare is mainly active at dusk and at night. During the day it remains in a shallow depression in the ground, known as a form, which is concealed among vegetation. It feeds on leaves, buds, roots, berries, fruit, fungi, bark, and twigs.

Snowshoe hare

The snowshoe hare is dark brown in summer, but its coat turns white in winter so that it can hide against the snow. Only the tips of its ears remain dark. This seasonal change of hair color helps the hare hide from enemies. Usually active at night and in the early morning, the snowshoe hare eats grass in summer and twigs and buds in winter.

Latin name	Lepus americanus
Size	Body: 17–20 in (42–50 cm)
Habitat	Forest, swamps, thickets
Distribution	Alaska, Canada, N. U.S.A.

Latin name	Lepus europaeus
Size	Body: 17–30 in (44–76 cm)
Habitat	Open country and woodland
Distribution	Europe, Asia; introduced: Australia, North and South America

European rabbit

European rabbits live together in a complex system of burrows called a warren. There may be up to 200 rabbits in a colony. Grass and leafy plants are their main food, but they also eat grain and can damage young trees. Females have several litters a year, with three to nine young in each litter.

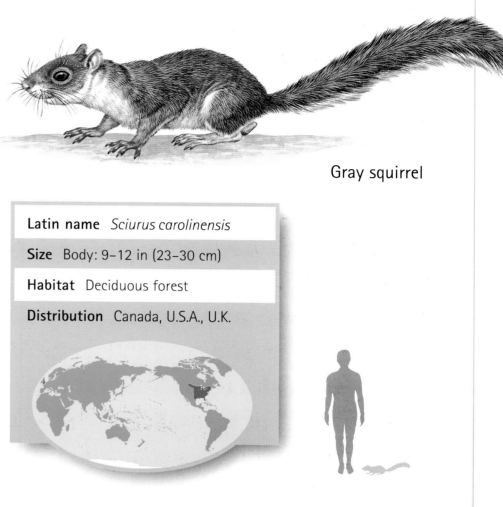

Gray squirrel

Latin name *Sciurus carolinensis*

Size Body: 9–12 in (23–30 cm)

Habitat Deciduous forest

Distribution Canada, U.S.A., U.K.

Latin name *Oryctolagus cuniculus*

Size Body: 14–18 in (35–45 cm)

Habitat Grassland and woodland

Distribution Europe, N.W. Africa; introduced: South America, Australia

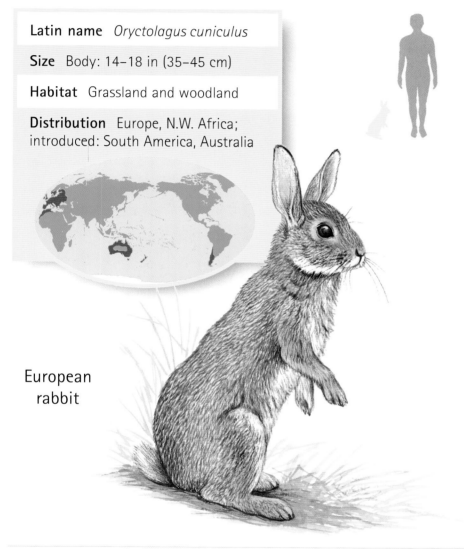

European rabbit

Gray squirrel

The gray squirrel's natural home is the oak, hickory, and walnut forests of eastern North America, where its numbers are controlled by owls, foxes, and bobcats. It feeds on seeds and nuts each day. It will also eat eggs, young birds, and insects. Occasionally, gray squirrels will also strip the bark from young trees to gain access to the nutritious sap beneath.

Black-tailed prairie dog

Prairie dogs live in huge burrows called towns. A town may house several thousand animals. They come out during the day to feed on grass and other plants. Feeding is interspersed by socializing, accompanied by chattering. Prairie dogs warn each other of any danger using sharp, doglike barks.

Latin name *Cynomys ludovicianus*

Size Body: 11–12 in (28–30 cm)

Habitat Grassland (prairie)

Distribution Central U.S.A.

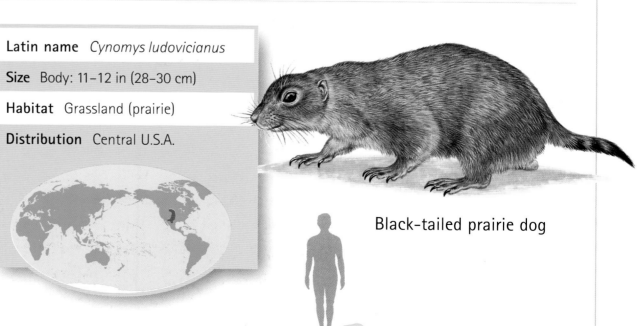

Black-tailed prairie dog

Shrews, mice, and rats

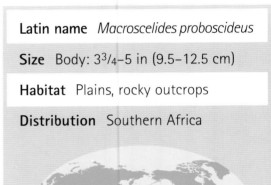

This group of rodents is made up of more than 900 different species. They are subdivided into those that are found in the Americas and are called New World rodents, and those that are found in Europe, Africa, and Asia and are called Old World rodents. Although they mainly eat plants, they will eat a wide range of foods. Some will also eat insects and even fish. Rodents such as the black rat and the house mouse have adapted to life alongside humans and some are considered a pest because they damage crops and property and have been linked to the spread of disease.

Short-eared elephant shrew

Latin name	*Macroscelides proboscideus*
Size	Body: 3³/₄–5 in (9.5–12.5 cm)
Habitat	Plains, rocky outcrops
Distribution	Southern Africa

Greater bandicoot rat

Greater bandicoot rat

These rodents are serious pests in many agricultural areas because they not only spoil grain but they also steal large quantities of food to store in their own underground larders. Greater bandicoot rats breed throughout the year and they can produce litters of 10 to 12 young each time.

Latin name	*Bandicota indica*
Size	Body 6¹/₂–14 in (16–36 cm)
Habitat	Forest and scrub
Distribution	India to S. China, S.E. Asia

Short-eared elephant shrew

Elephant shrews are named for their extraordinary, trunklike noses. They walk on all fours, but when they need to move fast, they hop on their back legs like miniature kangaroos. They live in dry, open country and they are active during both day and night. They feed on termites, seeds, fruit, and berries in the daytime, but find shelter from the midday sun in burrows.

Black rat

The black rat, also known as the house or ship rat, has carried with it such diseases as bubonic plague, typhus, and rabies. It is sometimes said to have altered human destiny more than any single man or woman. The success of this species is due to its extremely wide-ranging diet and its rapid rate of reproduction. Litters of up to 10 are born every six weeks or so.

Black rat

Latin name	*Rattus rattus*
Size	Body: 6$\frac{1}{2}$–10 in (16–26 cm)
Habitat	Associated with humans
Distribution	Worldwide

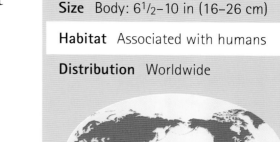

Fish-eating rat

Fish-eating rats have partially webbed feet that enable them to swim strongly through lakes and rivers. The upper incisor teeth are simple, spikelike structures used to spear fish, which are then dragged ashore for consumption. The rats produce one or two litters of young every year.

Latin name	*Mus musculus*
Size	Body: 2$\frac{1}{4}$–4 in (6–10 cm)
Habitat	Associated with humans
Distribution	Worldwide

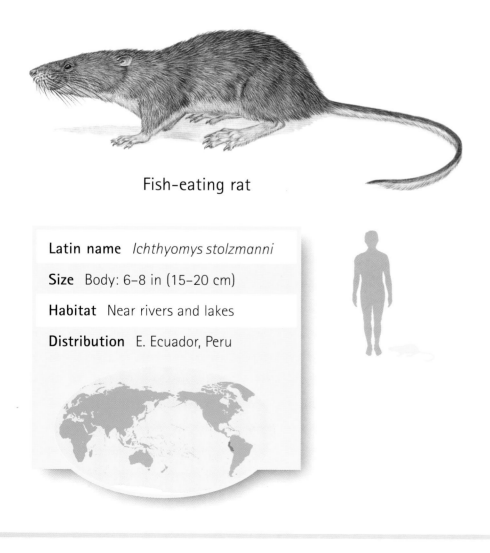

Fish-eating rat

Latin name	*Ichthyomys stolzmanni*
Size	Body: 6–8 in (15–20 cm)
Habitat	Near rivers and lakes
Distribution	E. Ecuador, Peru

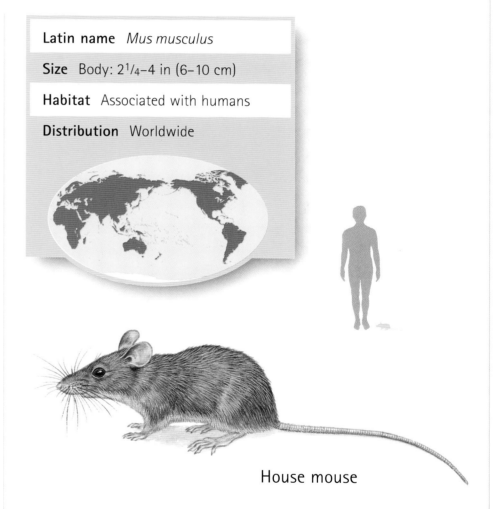

House mouse

House mouse

Mice eat relatively little, but they spoil vast quantities of stored food such as grain. Wild mice are nocturnal and have a very keen sense of hearing. They feed on grass seeds and plant stems and, occasionally, on insects. These rodents usually run about on all fours, but when they are eating or defending themselves they can stand on their hind legs, using their tails for support.

Lemurs, mouse-lemurs, and aye-aye

Lemurs, aye-ayes, bush babies, lorises, and tarsiers are primates found in parts of Africa and southern Asia. They have smaller brains than monkeys and apes. Lemurs and aye-ayes are found only on the island of Madagascar. The marmosets and tamarins of the South American rain forests are close relatives of the New World monkeys. They are among the most attractive primates, with colorful fur and unusual "hairstyles."

Latin name	Varecia variegata
Size	Body: 24 in (60 cm)
Habitat	Rain forest
Distribution	N.E. and E. Madagascar

Russet mouse-lemur

Ruffed lemur

Russet mouse-lemur

Mainly nocturnal in its habits, this tiny primate moves swiftly and nimbly on fine branches. It uses its long tail for balance and will leap across gaps between trees. It also comes down to the ground to forage in leaf litter for beetles. Its main food is insects and small vertebrates.

Latin name	Microcebus rufus
Size	Body: 5–6 in (12.5–15 cm)
Habitat	Forest
Distribution	E. Madagascar

Ruffed lemur

Distinguished by its long ruff, this lemur has either black-and-white fur or else is a striking chestnut red color, with black limbs and tail. It is a nimble climber and is most active at dusk and during the first part of the night, when it forages among the branches of trees for fruit, leaves, and bark. It rarely descends to the ground.

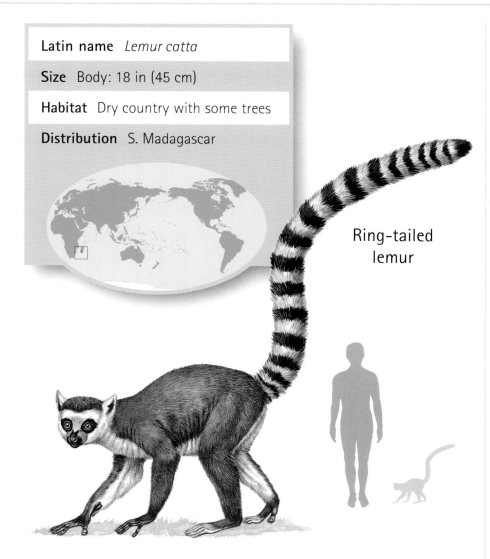

Latin name *Lemur catta*

Size Body: 18 in (45 cm)

Habitat Dry country with some trees

Distribution S. Madagascar

Ring-tailed
lemur

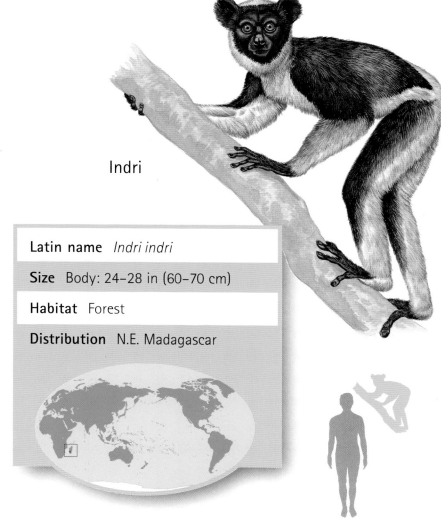

Indri

Latin name *Indri indri*

Size Body: 24–28 in (60–70 cm)

Habitat Forest

Distribution N.E. Madagascar

Ring-tailed lemur

The ring-tailed lemur climbs to the tops of trees to bathe in the early morning sunshine after a cold night. It marks its territory with smelly secretions from scent glands. During the mating season, two rival males will rub their tails with this scent and have a "stink fight" by wafting their smelly tails in the air at each other.

Indri

The indri is the largest of the lemurs, and is found in forests up to 6,000 ft (1,800 m) above sea level. It has a naked black face and a shortened snout. Indris live in family groups and are active during the day at all levels of the forest, looking for leaves, shoots, and fruit to eat. Females give birth to one young at a time.

Aye-aye

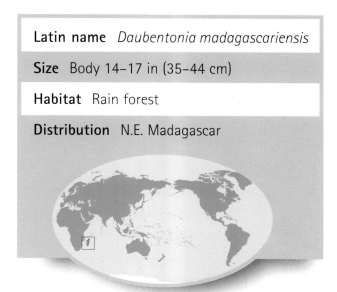

The aye-aye taps on trees with its long middle finger, listens for the sound of insects moving under the bark, and then uses the same finger to pull the insects out. Because local tradition says that seeing this strange-looking animal brings bad luck, it is often killed.

Aye-aye

Latin name *Daubentonia madagascariensis*

Size Body 14–17 in (35–44 cm)

Habitat Rain forest

Distribution N.E. Madagascar

Caring for young

Most mammals not only feed their young but also protect them during the early stages of life. Many also teach their young to forage and hunt for food for themselves and to avoid danger. Some adult mammals keep their young hidden in a den or secret place. If they are in danger, the mother may pick the young up in her mouth and carry them to safety.

Mother and teacher

The female cheetah is a caring mother. She guards her cubs watchfully and when they are about six months old, she starts to teach them how to hunt for their own food. She will even bring back live prey from a hunt so that her cubs can finish it off and so learn how to kill. The mother stays with her cubs until they are about 24 months old before leaving them to fend for themselves.

Below: A female cheetah gives birth to between two and eight cubs at a time. However, nearly 90 percent of these cubs will die before they reach adulthood.

Above: Grooming each other's fur is an important activity for animals such as monkeys. This mother is raking through her young's fur to remove dirt and fleas.

Right: Marsupials (*see* pages 14–16), such as kangaroos, give birth to live young that are very underdeveloped. These tiny creatures must crawl through the mother's fur into her pouch, where they can feed on the mother's milk and continue developing.

Kangaroo and developed young

Baby kangaroo in pouch

Raising young

Although many animal species take time to look after their young, few spend as much time and energy rearing and nuturing their offspring as mammals do. In many mammals, the young are able to move around as soon as they are born. For example, young horses are able to run around almost immediately after birth. This condition is called precocial. In other cases, the young are helpless. For example, dog puppies are born almost completely blind. This condition is called altricial. The parents of altricial young must spend a lot of time raising their young in the early stages.

Feeding young

A female mammal feeds her young on milk from her own body. She has special mammary glands that produce milk. The babies suck milk from teats, or nipples, on the mammary glands. The milk contains all the nourishment the babies need during the first few weeks of life. Animals such as pigs, which have large numbers of young, have many teats so they can feed all their babies at once.

WILD BOAR FEEDING ITS YOUNG

A pig may have as many as 20 young

Apes, gibbons, and monkeys

Humans, monkeys, and apes all belong to a group of about 250 species called primates. These mammals tend to have relatively large brains, making them intelligent and quick to learn new skills. Many primates have opposable thumbs, which means that their thumbs can move across their palms to press against their fingers, allowing them to grasp objects firmly. Some also have opposable big toes. Most primates live in trees, and they have forward-pointing eyes to help them judge the distances between branches.

Latin name	*Alouatta seniculus*
Size	Body: up to 28 in (70 cm)
Habitat	Forest, mangroves
Distribution	N. South America

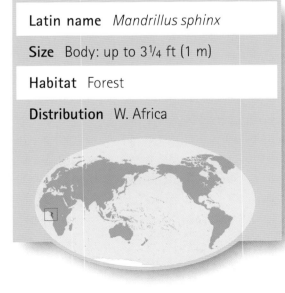

Red howler monkey

Mandrill

Mandrill

The forest-dwelling mandrill is unmistakable, with its red nose and blue cheeks. A female mandrill gives birth to a single baby, which she carries about with her, either on her back or clinging to her belly. One male guards a group of females and young as they forage for fruit, nuts, worms, and mushrooms.

Latin name	*Mandrillus sphinx*
Size	Body: up to 3¼ ft (1 m)
Habitat	Forest
Distribution	W. Africa

Red howler monkey

Red howler monkeys live in the rain forest in troops of as many as 30. Sometimes, all the males in a troop join together in a dawn chorus of howling that can be heard up to 3 miles (5 km) away. The howling tells other monkeys to stay away from their territory. The male howler monkey has a large throat, which has a special chamber that amplifies its call.

Lar gibbon

The lar gibbon lives in trees and rarely descends to the ground. It swings through the trees and runs upright along branches. At dawn, the gibbons start calling, or singing, with males and females alternating in duets. They live in small family groups.

Latin name *Hylobates lar*

Size Body: up to 25 in (65 cm)

Habitat Rain forest, dry forest

Distribution S. China, S.E. Asia

Lar gibbon

Chimpanzee

The chimpanzee mainly eats plants, but will occasionally eat insects and meat. It makes many noises, gestures, and facial expressions. It has learned to use some objects as simple tools. For example, stones are used to smash open nuts, wads of leaves to mop up drinking water, and sticks to pry grubs out of rotten wood.

Chimpanzee

Latin name *Pan Troglodytes*

Size Height: up to 5½ ft (1.7 m)

Habitat Rain forest, savanna

Distribution W. and central Africa

Latin name *Gorilla gorilla*

Size Height: up to 6 ft (1.8 m)

Habitat Rain forest

Distribution W. and central Africa

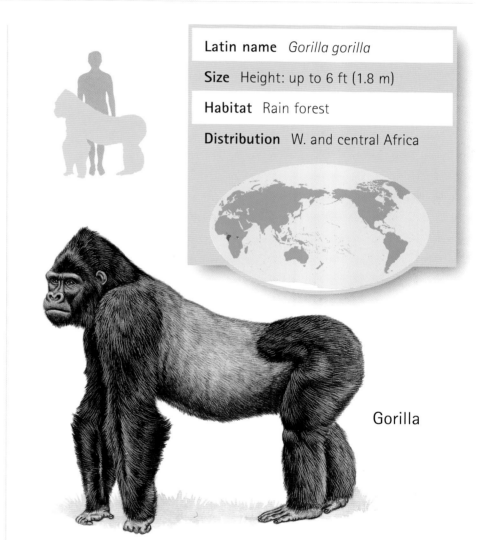

Gorilla

Gorilla

Gorillas spend most of their time on the ground. They feed on leaves, buds, stalks, berries, bark, and ferns. They live in troops of as many as 30 animals, made up of a leading adult male, a few young males, and several females and their young. Young gorillas travel on their mother's back until they are two or three years old.

Bats

Bats are the only mammals to have evolved true flight. They power themselves through the air on smooth wings of skin, making sudden midair turns and spectacular twists. Most bats spend the day asleep, hanging upside down, out of reach of predators. At night, they are ready to launch themselves into the air to hunt for food. Some bats use echolocation to find their food and navigate in the dark, making high-pitched sounds that bounce, or echo, off objects and are picked up by the bats' ears. The bats use the echoes to locate their prey and avoid obstacles.

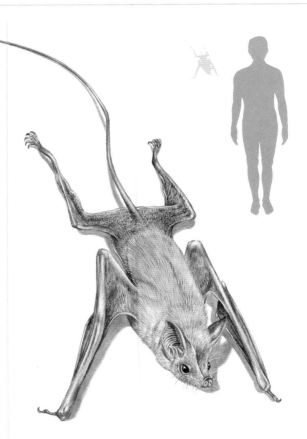

Greater mouse-tailed bat

Latin name	*Rhinopoma microphyllum*
Size	Wingspan: 7–10 in (18–25 cm)
Habitat	Treeless arid land
Distribution	W. Africa to India and Sumatra

Greater fruit bat

Greater fruit bat

The largest wings in the bat world belong to the greater fruit bat. They fly at dusk to find fruit to eat or sweet flower nectar to lap up. They help fruit trees reproduce by carrying pollen, which sticks to the bats' fur, from flower to flower. Fruit seeds that the bats spit out or pass in their droppings take root and grow into new fruit trees.

Latin name	*Pteropus giganteus*
Size	Wingspan: 5 ft (1.5 m)
Habitat	Forest, scrub
Distribution	S. and S.E. Asia

Greater mouse-tailed bat

Colonies of greater mouse-tailed bats occupy roosts in large ruined buildings. They feed exclusively on insects and, in those areas where a cool season temporarily depletes the food supply, the bats may enter a deep sleep resembling torpor. They can survive like this for many weeks without eating or drinking.

Greater false vampire

The greater false vampire regularly supplements its diet of insects, spiders, and other invertebrates with prey such as other bats, rodents, frogs, and even fish. Groups of between 3 and 50 false vampires roost together and are usually the sole inhabitants of their caves. Presumably their hunting tendencies deter other bats from sharing their home.

Latin name	*Megaderma lyra*
Size	Wingspan: 9–12 in (23–30 cm)
Habitat	Forest, open land
Distribution	India to S.E. Asia

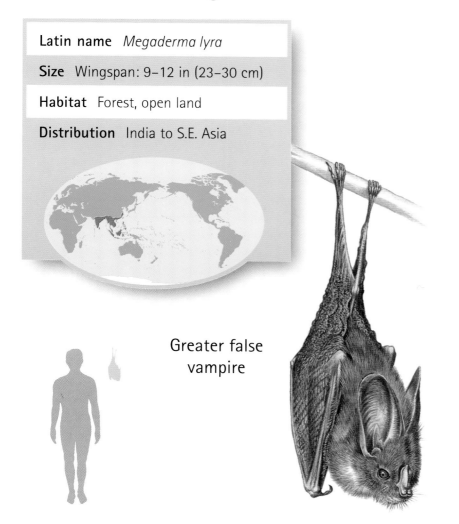

Greater false vampire

Latin name	*Rhinolophus ferrumequinum*
Size	Wingspan: 13–14 in (33–35 cm)
Habitat	Forest, open land, and farmland
Distribution	Europe, Asia, N. Africa

Greater horseshoe bat

Greater horseshoe bat

The greater horseshoe bat feeds on beetles, swooping down to snatch them off the ground with pinpoint accuracy. It roosts in caves, trees, and the roofs of old buildings. But as caves are explored, trees cut down, and buildings leveled, it is harder and harder for the bats to find suitable homes. Its numbers are declining in northwestern Europe.

Common pipistrelle

Perhaps the commonest of European bats, pipistrelle bats roost in large groups containing up to a thousand or more in lofts, church spires, farm buildings, and the like. In winter, these bats migrate to a suitable dry cave to hibernate in colonies of 100,000 or more. They feed on insects, eating small prey in flight, but taking larger catches to a perch to eat.

Common pipistrelle

Latin name	*Pipistrellus pipistrellus*
Size	Wingspan: 7–10 in (18–25 cm)
Habitat	Open land
Distribution	Europe, east to Kashmir

Dogs, hyenas, and wolves

Gray wolf

All domestic dogs are descended from wolves. Wolves and other wild dogs have long legs for chasing prey and sharp teeth for killing it. A dog's most important sensory organ is its nose, which it uses to detect the scent of prey, find a mate, and identify other animals. They can even tell whether another animal is afraid or relaxed. Wild dogs hunt animals as small as mice and as large as moose. Some wild dogs, such as foxes, live on their own. Others, such as wolves and hunting dogs, live, travel, and hunt in groups called packs.

Latin name	Canis lupus
Size	Body: up to 6½ ft (2 m)
Habitat	Tundra, steppe, forest
Distribution	North America, Russia, N. Europe

Coyote

Coyote

A highly adaptable animal, the coyote has managed to thrive, even to increase its population, despite being trapped and poisoned for many years. Although the coyote probably does kill some farm animals, its diet consists mainly of rodents and rabbits. It also eats snakes, insects, carrion, fruit, berries, and grasses.

Latin name	Canis latrans
Size	Body: up to 3½ ft (1.1 m)
Habitat	Prairies, open woodland
Distribution	North America, Central America

Gray wolf

The largest of all the wild dogs, the gray wolf preys on hoofed mammals, such as bison, moose, and musk-oxen. Packs vary in size from 5 to 20 dogs, led by the strongest male. Each pack has its own hunting territory that can cover up to 386 square miles (1,000 square km) or more. The wolves howl loudly to warn other packs to stay away.

Red fox

The red fox has adapted to many different environments, from forests and grasslands to mountains, deserts, and even towns and cities. Red foxes live and hunt alone and come together only to breed and rear their young. They usually prey on rodents, rabbits, and other small animals, but they will also eat fruit, vegetables, and fish.

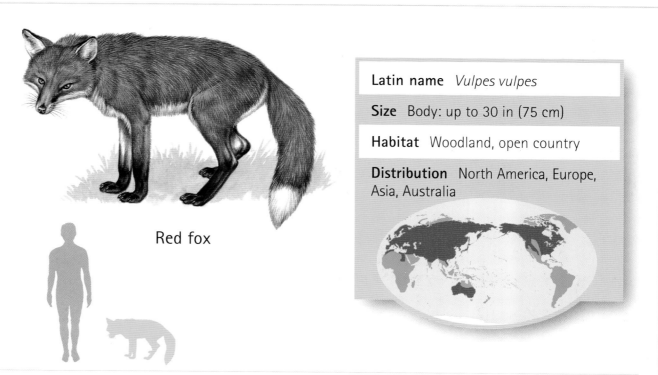

Red fox

Latin name	*Vulpes vulpes*
Size	Body: up to 30 in (75 cm)
Habitat	Woodland, open country
Distribution	North America, Europe, Asia, Australia

Latin name	*Chrysocyon brachyurus*
Size	Body: 4¼ ft (1.3 m)
Habitat	Grassland, swamp edge
Distribution	South America

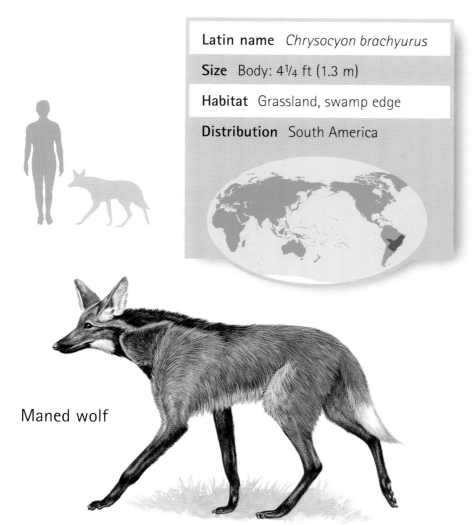

Maned wolf

Maned wolf

The maned wolf is similar to the red fox in appearance, but with longer legs and a longer muzzle. It has also an erectile mane on its neck and shoulders. A wary creature, the maned wolf lives in remote areas and hunts mainly at night. It eats large rodents, birds, reptiles, frogs, insects, snails, fruit, and plants.

Hunting dog

Hunting dogs hunt together as a pack. The pack chases a group of animals, such as wildebeest, separates one from the fleeing herd, and then moves in for the kill. These dogs once hunted throughout the African savanna. But because so many were shot by farmers, today the dogs are found in only a few scattered places.

Latin name	*Lycaon pictus*
Size	Body: up to 4½ ft (1.4 m)
Habitat	Savanna, semidesert
Distribution	Africa, south of Sahara

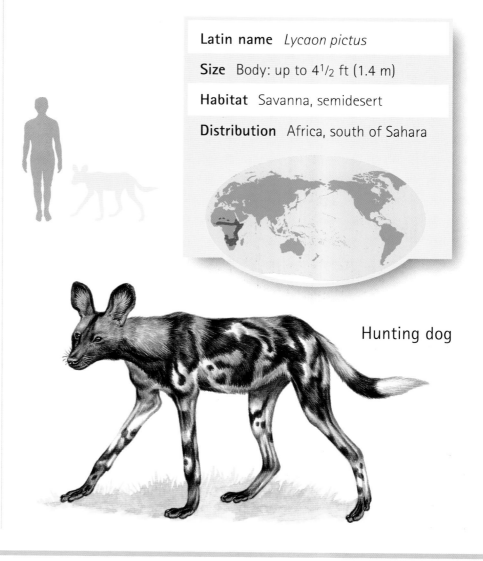

Hunting dog

Bears, pandas, and raccoons

Sun bear

Both the bear and raccoon families developed from doglike ancestors millions of years ago. Bears are the largest flesh-eating land mammals, but they will eat almost anything, including plants and insects. Raccoons—and their relatives the coatis and olingos—are long-tailed carnivores that like to spend much of their time in trees. There are two different types of panda: the giant panda is sometimes classified with the bear, and the red panda with the raccoon.

Brown bear

Latin name	*Helarctos malayanus*
Size	Body: up to 5 ft (1.5 m)
Habitat	Mountain, lowland forest
Distribution	S.E. Asia

Sun bear

The sun bear is the smallest bear species, with a strong, stocky body and powerful jaws. It spends the day in a nest in a tree, sleeping and sunbathing. It searches for food at night, using its long tongue to lick honey out of bees' nests and termites from their mounds. With its curved claws it hooks fruit from branches and tears off tree bark to uncover tasty grubs.

Brown bear

Also known as the grizzly bear, the brown bear eats mostly leaves, berries, fruit, nuts, and roots and sometimes insects, rodents, and fish. It also hunts large mammals such as moose and musk oxen. The brown bear may hide its dead prey under dirt and leaves until it is ready to eat it.

Latin name	*Ursus arctos*
Size	Body: up to 9 ft (2.7 m)
Habitat	Forest, tundra
Distribution	Europe, Asia, North America

Raccoon

Latin name *Ursus maritimus*

Size Body: up to 8 ft (2.5 m)

Habitat Coasts, ice floes

Distribution Ice-covered Arctic regions

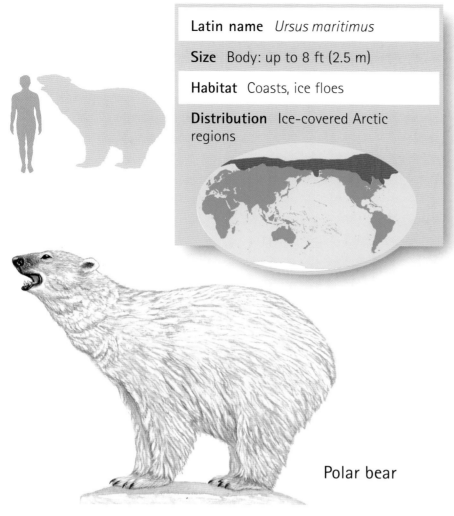
Polar bear

Polar bear

With a thick layer of specially insulated fur to keep it warm, a polar bear is perfectly comfortable roaming across the Arctic ice in freezing temperatures. Cubs are born in dens dug by their mother in deep snow. They stay with her for about 28 months, learning how to hunt seals and to fight.

Raccoon

The raccoon runs and climbs well and swims if necessary. It is most active at night. As well as catching prey such as frogs, fish, mice, and birds, it often raids garbage cans, searching for edible items with its long, sensitive fingers. It has a peculiar habit of washing food before eating it.

Latin name *Procyon lotor*

Size Body: 20–30 in (50–75 cm)

Habitat Wooded areas, swamps

Distribution Canada to Panama

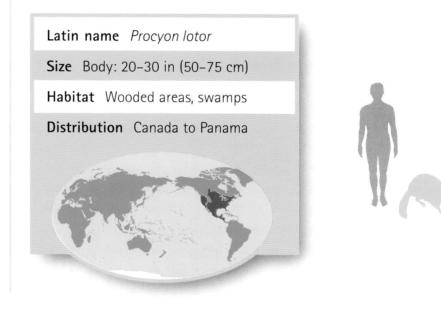

Giant panda

Latin name *Ailuropoda melanoleuca*

Size Body: up to 6 ft (1.8 m)

Habitat Bamboo forest

Distribution Central China

Giant panda

The giant panda has to feed for up to 12 hours each day to survive. During that time it consumes up to 28 pounds (12.5 kg) of bamboo. The panda has a thumblike bone in each hand that allows it to grip its food. Pandas are primarily ground-dwelling but climb trees for shelter or refuge. There are only about 1,000 giant pandas left in the wild.

Civets and mongooses

Latin name	*Prionodon linsang*
Size	Body 15–17 in (38–44 cm)
Habitat	Forest
Distribution	S.E. Asia

These mammals are small to medium-size carnivores. The 34 or so species of civets are tree-dwelling hunters that are active at night. They live in southwestern Europe, Africa, and Asia. Most have large, pointed ears on the top of the head, and five toes with claws and at least partial webbing. There are 39 species of mongooses. These fast-moving ground dwellers live in Africa and Asia. They have long, cylindrical bodies that are well adapted to chasing prey—such as insects, scorpions, and small vertebrates—down burrows.

Banded linsang

African palm civet

African palm civet

This civet has short legs and a long, thick tail. It is a skilled climber and spends much of its life in trees, where it rests during the day. It usually hunts at night, catching insects and small animals such as lizards and birds. It also eats many kinds of fruit and leaves. The female gives birth to litters of two or three young at any time of the year.

Latin name	*Nandinia binotata*
Size	Body: 17–24 in (44–60 cm)
Habitat	Forest, savanna, woodland
Distribution	Central Africa

Banded linsang

The slender, graceful banded linsang varies from whitish-gray to brownish-gray in color, with four or five dark bands across its back and dark spots on its sides and legs. It is nocturnal and spends much of its life in trees, where it climbs and jumps skillfully, but it is just as agile on the ground. It hunts birds, small mammals, insects, lizards, and frogs and also eats birds' eggs.

Fanalouc

Fanalouc

Active at dusk and during the night, the fanalouc does not climb or jump well, but slowly hops along the ground, searching for earthworms, insects, snails, and frogs. When food is abundant, it stores fat near the base of its tail to live on during the dry season.

Latin name	*Eupleres goudotii*
Size	Body: 20–24 in (50–60 cm)
Habitat	Rain forest, swamps
Distribution	N. Madagascar

Latin name	*Suricata suricatta*
Size	Body: 10–14 in (25–35 cm)
Habitat	Open country, savanna
Distribution	Southern Africa

Indian mongoose

The Indian mongoose sleeps in a burrow at night, and hunts during the day. It eats almost any food it can catch, including snakes, scorpions, and insects. It is popular among humans because it hunts pests such as rats and mice. As a result, the Indian mongoose has been introduced into areas outside its normal range.

Meerkat

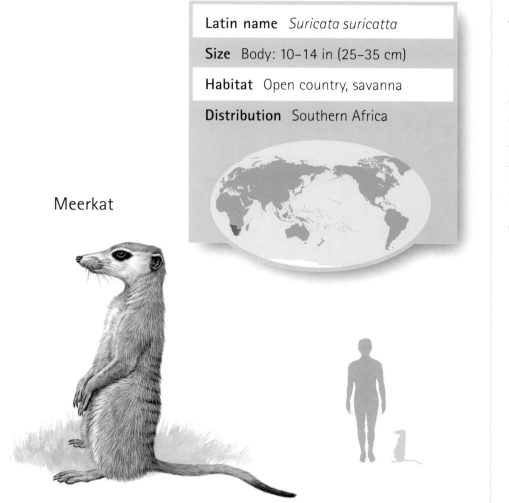

Indian mongoose

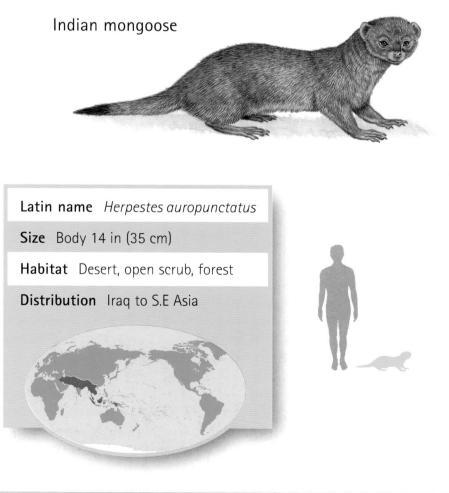

Meerkat

The meerkat has the long body and short legs typical of many mongooses. Meerkats are gregarious and live in burrows in groups of up to 30. They forage in pairs or small groups during the day, eating small animals, roots, and fruit. They will take turns foraging and sitting up on their hindlegs to watch for danger.

Latin name	*Herpestes auropunctatus*
Size	Body 14 in (35 cm)
Habitat	Desert, open scrub, forest
Distribution	Iraq to S.E Asia

The big cats

Pair of lions

The big cats are the eight species of large wild cats, including lions, tigers, leopards, pumas, and jaguars. Big cats may live and hunt on their own, like leopards, or in groups, like lions. They are found on every continent except Australia and Antarctica, and live in many habitats, from lions in sub-Saharan Africa to tigers in chilly Siberia.

Above: Lions live and hunt together in groups, or prides, of two or three adult males, up to 15 females, and their young.

Hunting

The big cats are expert hunters. Their strong legs enable them to catch their prey in a brief, rapid chase or with a lightning-quick pounce. They have flexible backbones that allow them to twist and turn easily when chasing prey. When they pounce, their claws extend and grip their victim's flesh.

Habitats

The big cats have adapted to many different habitats. The jaguar (right) lives in tropical forests in North and South America, climbing trees to lie in wait for its prey, as does the leopard in Africa and Asia. Lions and cheetahs live in the hot open savanna in Africa. The Siberian tiger is found in the cold forests of eastern Russia and North Korea, while the snow leopard lives in mountain meadows in central Asia.

Breeding

Below: A cheetah closes in on its prey. The cheetah is the fastest land animal, capable of speeds of 69 mph (112 km/h), but it tires quickly, so must first get close to its prey before its high-speed pounce.

Lions are the only big cats to live in a large pride. This means that the group can go off to hunt and leave all the cubs behind with one or two adults. A female will then return and lead the cubs to the kill. The female cubs will stay with the pride for life, while the males are driven out at around 18 months of age. In the case of solitary big cats, such as leopards, jaguars, and cheetahs, males and females come together only briefly to breed and then the female rears the cubs on her own.

Below: The female tiger gives birth to a litter of between two and six cubs. The young may stay with their mother for two or three years as she teaches them the hunting skills they will need as adults. The father takes no part in their rearing.

Cubs are taught to hunt by their mother   Tiger mother and cubs

Cats

There are approximately 36 species in the cat family. Of all the predators, cats are probably the most efficient killers. Coloring, size, and fur patterning vary within the family, but all the species, small and large, are basically similar in appearance and proportions to the domestic cat. Cat bodies are muscular and flexible. Their powerful limbs have long, sharp, completely retractile claws on the feet for grasping prey—except for the cheetah, in which the claws do not retract, giving better grip. Cat eyes are large and forward-facing. All this makes cats dangerous predators.

Tiger

Tiger

The largest of the big cats, the tiger has a massive, muscular body and powerful limbs. Males and females look similar, but males have longer, more prominent cheek whiskers. Tigers are generally shy, nocturnal creatures and usually live alone, although they are not unsociable and are on amicable terms with their neighbors.

Lion

Lion

The lion is powerfully built, with a broad head, thick, strong legs, and a long tail tipped with a tuft of hair that conceals a clawlike spine. The male is larger than the female and has a heavy mane, which may be light yellow to black, on its neck and shoulders. Lions spend 20 hours or more resting each day, and hunt during the day and night.

Latin name	*Panthera leo*
Size	Body: up to 8 ft (2.4 m)
Habitat	Open savanna
Distribution	Sub-saharan Africa

Latin name	*Panthera tigris*
Size	Body: 6–11 ft (1.8–3.3 m)
Habitat	Forest
Distribution	Siberia to Java and Bali

Cheetah

The cheetah is the fastest of the big cats, able to reach speeds of more than 60 mph (100 km/h). Its body is long and supple, with high, muscular shoulders. Its long tail aids balance during the cheetah's fast turns. Cheetahs will stalk their prey before attacking with a short, rapid chase.

Latin name	*Acinonyx jubatus*
Size	Body: up to 4½ ft (1.4 m)
Habitat	Desert and savanna
Distribution	Africa, east to Asia

Latin name	*Felix silvestris*
Size	Body: 20–25 in (50–65 cm)
Habitat	Forest, scrub, and savanna
Distribution	Europe, Africa to India

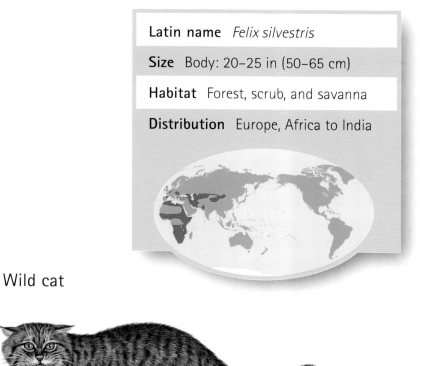

Wild cat

Cheetah

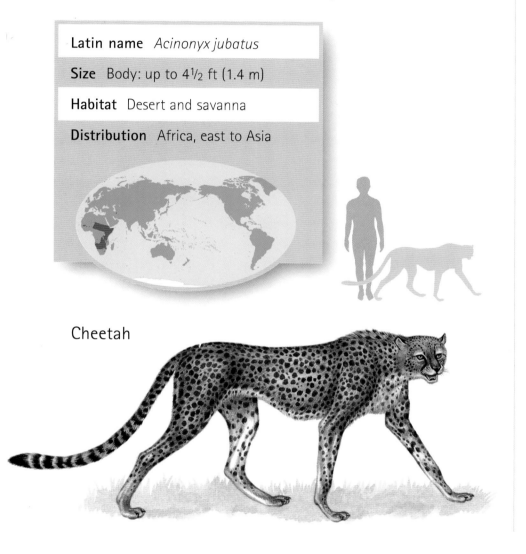

Wild cat

One of the ancestors of the domestic cat, the wild cat is similar in form but slightly larger, with a thicker tail, which is encircled with black rings. There are several distinct populations. Largely solitary and nocturnal, the wild cat lives in a well-defined territory. It stalks most of its prey on the ground, catching small rodents and birds.

Snow leopard

The snow leopard inhabits the alpine meadows high up in mountainous areas, amid snow and glaciers. It preys on wild sheep and goats. Its broad, furry feet stop it from sinking into the snow. It can make huge leaps between rocky crags, using its tail for balance.

Latin name	*Uncia uncia*
Size	Body: up to 5 ft (1.5 m)
Habitat	Mountain slopes, forest
Distribution	Pakistan, east to China

Snow leopard

Seals and sea lions

Seals and sea lions have bodies adapted to life in the water. With their torpedo-like bodies, these marine mammals are skillful swimmers and divers. They spend much of their time underwater, often diving to great depths in search of food. But because they have lungs, not gills like fish, they have to surface regularly to breathe air. They can slow down their heartbeat during dives to enable them to stay underwater for long periods. Seals and walruses swim by propelling themselves through the water with their taillike hind flippers, but sea lions use their long front flippers.

California sea lion

Latin name	*Zalophus californianus*
Size	Up to 7½ ft (2.2 m)
Habitat	Coasts and islands
Distribution	E. North Pacific

Northern fur seal

Northern fur seal

Northern fur seals have large rear flippers and feed on fish and squid, either alone or in pairs. They rarely come to land except to breed. The male may be four times the size of the female. The female gives birth to one young and stays with it for seven days before going off on brief feeding trips, returning to suckle the cub at intervals.

Latin name	*Callorhinus ursinus*
Size	Up to 6 ft (1.8 m)
Habitat	Breeds on islands
Distribution	Bering Sea, Okhotsk Sea

California sea lion

This is the fastest swimmer of all the seals and sea lions, capable of speeds of 25 mph (40 km/h). It can also move fast on land by turning its back flippers forward and lifting its body. In the breeding season, huge colonies gather on the rocky southwestern shores of the United States. Males arrive first and establish territories when the females start to give birth.

Leopard seal

The leopard seal is the fiercest hunter of all seals, with large tooth-studded jaws for grasping prey and tearing it apart. The leopard seal preys on penguins by catching them underwater just after they launch themselves off the ice. It also hunts smaller seals as well as fish, squid, and shellfish.

Latin name	*Hydrurga leptonyx*
Size	8–11 ft (2.4–3.4 m)
Habitat	Pack ice, coasts, islands
Distribution	Southern Ocean

Leopard seal

Gray seal

The male gray seal has massive shoulders and an elongated snout, while the female is smaller and has a flatter profile. They travel far from their breeding sites, but stay mostly in coastal waters, feeding on fish, squid, and octopus. Females arrive first at breeding sites and give birth before the males appear to establish positions on the beach.

Latin name	*Odobenus rosmarus*
Size	Up to 13 ft (4 m)
Habitat	Pack ice, rocky islands
Distribution	Arctic Ocean

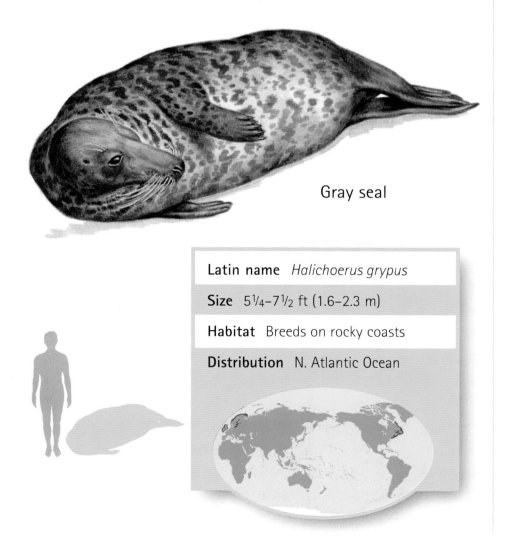

Gray seal

Latin name	*Halichoerus grypus*
Size	5¼–7½ ft (1.6–2.3 m)
Habitat	Breeds on rocky coasts
Distribution	N. Atlantic Ocean

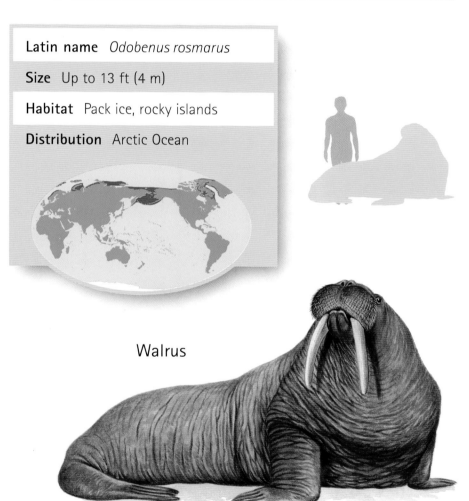

Walrus

Walrus

Walruses are huge animals that live in the Arctic, where they feed on shellfish. They have sharp tusks, which they use to drag themselves out of the water and for fighting, and thick skin, which protects them against injury. Their four flat flippers make them excellent swimmers. On land, walruses move with great difficulty. They spend much of their time sleeping on the ice in large groups.

Aardvark and pigs

Aardvark

Pigs are hoofed, omnivorous animals. There are nine species of pig, found in Europe, Asia, and Africa. They are stocky animals, with long heads and mobile flattened-out snouts they use to root for food. The upper canine teeth usually form tusks. Each foot has four toes, but only the third and fourth reach the ground and form hooves. The aardvark is the only mammal in its order (*see* pages 10–11) and is specially adapted to rooting out and eating insects. Like pigs, it has a long snout and an excellent sense of smell.

Bush pig

Aardvark

The aardvark is solitary and nocturnal. Its sight is poor, but its other senses are excellent. It has highly specialized nostrils surrounded by dense hair, which seals them off when the aardvark digs. It uses its powerful forelimbs to excavate burrows for shelter and to smash the nests of ants and termites, allowing it to sweep up the insects using its long, sticky tongue.

Bush pig

Bush pigs live in small groups of up to 12, led by an old male. They eat almost anything, including grass, roots, fruit, small mammals, birds, and carrion. Normally active during the day, they are nocturnal in areas where they are hunted. Bush pigs breed throughout the year, particularly when food is abundant.

Latin name	*Potamochoerus porcus*
Size	Body: 3¼–5 ft (1–1.5 m)
Habitat	Forest, bush, swamps
Distribution	Sub-Saharan Africa

Latin name	*Orycteropus afer*
Size	Body: 3¼–5¼ ft (1–1.6 m)
Habitat	All regions with termites
Distribution	Sub-Saharan Africa

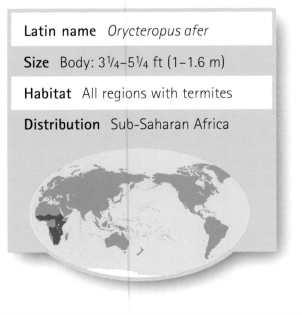

Warthog

The warthog has long legs, curving tusks, and a long, broad head with two pairs of large, wartlike protuberances. It lives in small family groups on the African savanna and on treeless plains, where it feeds on short grasses and herbs. In the hottest part of the day, it rests in its burrow, which is often the abandoned home of an aardvark.

Babirusa

Latin name	*Phacochoerus aethiopicus*
Size	Body: 3½–4½ ft (1.1–1.4 m)
Habitat	Savanna, treeless open plains
Distribution	Sub-Saharan Africa

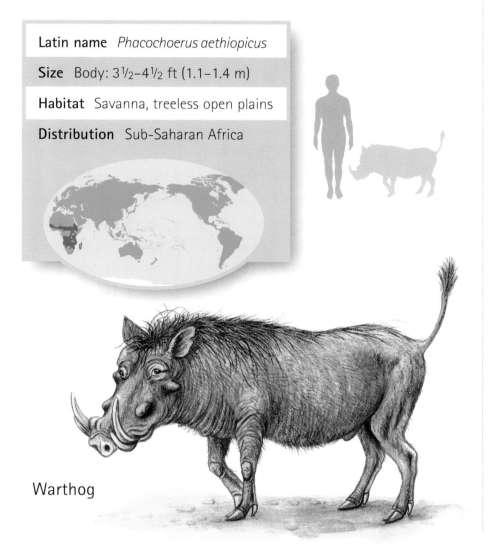

Warthog

Babirusa

Elusive animals, babirusas prefer to forage in dense cover near water. They are fast runners and good swimmers, even in the sea. They move in small groups, the male doing most of the rooting and unearthing of food, while females and young trail behind, feeding on items such as roots, berries, tubers, and leaves.

Latin name	*Babyrousa babyrussa*
Size	Body: 34–43 in (85–110 cm)
Habitat	Lake shores and river banks
Distribution	Sulawesi, Sula Islands

Wild boar

The wild boar is the ancestor of the farmyard pig. It lives alone or in groups of up to 20. Males stay separate from, but close to, the females. With its long snout, it roots around the woodland floor for plants and insects to eat. It also digs up bulbs and tubers. Young boars have striped coats that blend in with the trees and hide them from predators.

Wild boar

Latin name	*Sus scrofa*
Size	Body: 3½–4¼ ft (1.1–1.3 m)
Habitat	Forest, woodland
Distribution	Europe, Asia, N.W. Africa

Camels, deer, and horses

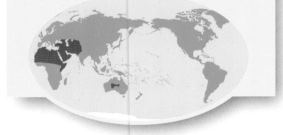

Camels and deer have an even number of toes and are all cud-chewers, which means that they have complex stomachs. When they eat, they first briefly chew leaves and grasses and swallow them. The animal then brings the partly digested food, called the cud, back up into its mouth and chews it again. Animals in the horse family, including zebras and donkeys, live in herds and feed mainly on grass. Their feet have only one toe with a single hoof on the end. This enables them to run very swiftly.

Dromedary camel

Przewlski's wild horse

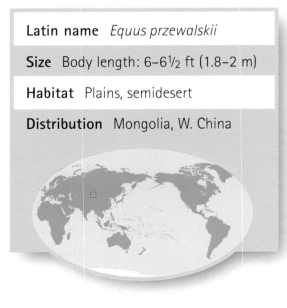

Przewlski's wild horse

This short, sturdy horse was the last true wild horse. It has not been seen in the wild since 1968 and now lives only in captivity. It was once common on the dry plains of Mongolia, where it grazed on grass and leaves. They have an erect mane and no forelock. They live in small herds, each led by a dominant male.

Latin name	*Equus przewalskii*
Size	Body length: 6–6½ ft (1.8–2 m)
Habitat	Plains, semidesert
Distribution	Mongolia, W. China

Latin name	*Camelus dromedarius*
Size	Body length: up to 11 ft (3.4 m)
Habitat	Desert, plains
Distribution	N. Africa, Middle East, Australia

Dromedary camel

The dromedary, or one-humped camel, now exists only as a domesticated animal. There are two main types: a heavily built animal used as a beast of burden, and a light, fast-running racer used for riding. It uses its hump as a fat store, which it can then live on when food is scarce. It can also go for long periods without drinking.

Grevy's Zebra

Latin name	*Equus grevyi*
Size	Body length: up to 9 ft (2.7 m)
Habitat	Savanna, semidesert
Distribution	E. Africa

This species has the narrowest stripes of all zebras and lives in drier regions than most. It eats tough grasses, grazing during the day and resting in shade in the noon heat. Mature males live alone, each in his own territory, while males without a territory form troops. Females and young live in separate troops of a dozen or more.

Zebra

Forest musk deer

The male musk deer has a scent gland on the underside of its body. This oozes a strong-smelling liquid called musk, which the deer uses to send signals to females in the breeding season. The musk deer has a coat of long, thick, bristly hairs and two tusklike teeth on its upper jaw. It feeds on lichens, buds, shoots, grass, and twigs.

Latin name	*Moschus chrysogaster*
Size	Body length: about 3¼ ft (1 m)
Habitat	High-altitude forest
Distribution	Himalayas to C. China

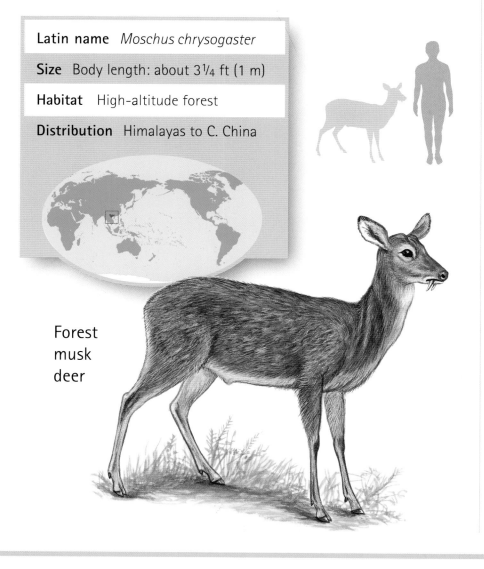

Forest musk deer

Latin name	*Rangifer tarandus*
Size	Body length: up to 7½ ft (2.2 m)
Habitat	Tundra
Distribution	N. Europe, Asia, North America

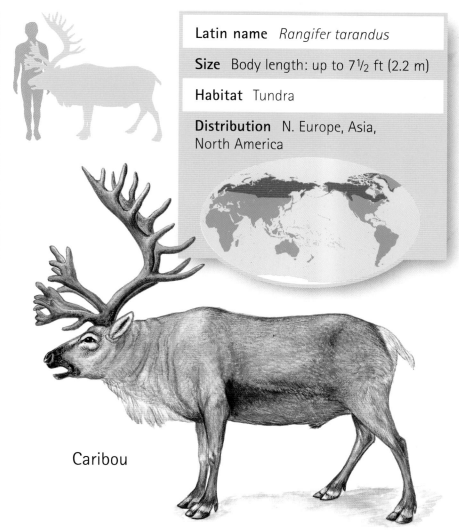

Caribou

Caribou

The caribou, or reindeer, is the only deer species in which both males and females have antlers. In other species only males have them. It feeds mainly on lichens in winter. In summer, many herds travel north to feed on the rich grass and plants of the tundra. Females and young live in herds, but males often live separately.

Whale groups

There are two kinds of whales, toothed and baleen. Toothed whales include dolphins, porpoises, and smaller whales, such as killer and sperm whales. They eat fish and other prey. Baleen whales, such as the huge blue and humpback whales, have bristly plates instead of teeth in their mouths and feed on tiny fish and plankton.

Below: A humpback whale leaps out of the water in a movement known as "breaching." Scientists believe that whales may sometimes breach as a form of play.

Streamlined body helps fast movement through the water.

Killer whale

Toothed Whales

Toothed whales include more than 67 species of small whale, dolphin, and porpoise, including the killer whale. All toothed whales prey on fish and squid, and the killer whale also hunts larger prey such as seals, sea lions, and other whales. Sperm whales also hunt giant squid. To help locate their prey, toothed whales use a form of ultrasonic sonar: they emit high-frequency clicking sounds that bounce off objects, the echoes informing the whale with astonishing accuracy of the size, distance, and speed of travel of the object. All of these whales have teeth; some a pair, some as many as 200.

Baleen Plates

In some whales, the baleen plates used to filter tiny creatures out of the water can be up to 15 ft (4.5 m) long. In order to feed, the whale traps a huge amount of water in its mouth. It then squeezes its mouth to force the water out and catches its tiny prey, known as plankton, on the fine fringes of the baleen plate. During the summer months, a large blue whale may eat 4 tons of tiny krill every day.

Baleen Whales

The baleen whales include the ten largest whales—as well as the largest creature on the planet, the blue whale. These marine giants feed on tiny planktonic animals, which they extract from the sea by filtering water through "baleen plates" of fringed horny material hanging from their upper jaws. There are three families of baleen whale: rorquals, gray, and right whales. Hunted to the brink of extinction, many species of whales are now protected by international law, and the numbers of some species are steadily increasing.

The baby, or calf, is about 13 ft (4 m) long.

Sperm whale and calf

Above: Whales are born in water. When a female gives birth, she is usually surrounded by other females, waiting to assist her and to help the newborn. Once born, the whale calf is pushed to the surface to take its first breath.

47

Whales and dolphins

There are more than 80 species of whale, dolphin, and porpoise, which all belong to the order called cetaceans. Like sea cows and manatees, all cetaceans are mammals that spend their entire lives in water. They are streamlined and have strong tails, known as flukes. Their front limbs are modified into flippers, and there are no visible hind limbs.

Sperm whale

Humpback whale

Humpback whale

The humpback whale is famous for the amazingly complex songs it sings to keep in touch with other whales and to attract mates. This baleen whale often sings for hours on end, pausing only to breathe. These songs travel great distances through the water. Humpback whales feed in the polar regions in summer.

Latin name	*Megaptera novaeangeliae*
Size	48–62 ft (15–19 m)
Habitat	Oceans, coastal waters
Distribution	Worldwide

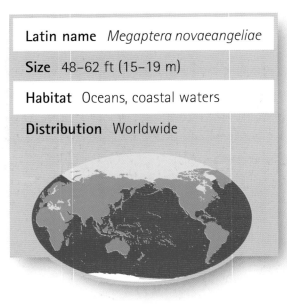

Latin name	*Physeter catodon*
Size	36–66 ft (11–20 m)
Habitat	Oceans
Distribution	Worldwide

Sperm whale

The largest of the toothed whales, the sperm whale has a huge head, which is one third of its total body weight. It can dive as deep as 3,300 ft (1,000 m), taking water into its huge nasal cavities to maintain buoyancy. It feeds mainly on deepwater squid, which it locates in the dark depths using sonar.

Blue whale

The largest animal that
has ever existed, the blue whale
can weigh up to 215 tons. This giant baleen whale feeds on huge
quantities of tiny shrimplike creatures called krill, eating 4 tons each
day in the summer. The blue whale is in danger of extinction. There
are only a few thousand left in the world's oceans.

Blue whale

Latin name	Balaenoptera musculus
Size	82–105 ft (25–32 m)
Habitat	Open ocean
Distribution	Worldwide

Ganges dolphin

One of only five species of freshwater dolphin,
the Ganges dolphin lives in muddy rivers in South
Asia. It has very poor eyesight—its eyes have no
lenses—and uses echolocation to find its food (fish
and shrimp). An agile animal, it generally swims on
its side, returning to the normal upright position to
breathe. Ganges dolphins usually travel in pairs.

Ganges dolphin

Latin name	Platanista gangetica
Size	5–7³/₄ ft (1.5–2.4 m)
Habitat	Forest
Distribution	India and Bangladesh

Common dolphin

This beautifully marked dolphin has pointed
flippers, a curved fin, and a long beak. It lives in
groups of between 20 and 100 animals. Several
dolphins will join together to help injured or sick
companions. These inquisitive sea mammals are
often seen swimming alongside ships, leaping and
rolling in the waves. They feed on fish and squid.

Common dolphin

Latin name	Delphinus delphis
Size	7–8¹/₂ ft (2.1–2.6 m)
Habitat	Coastal and oceanic waters
Distribution	Temperate, tropical oceans

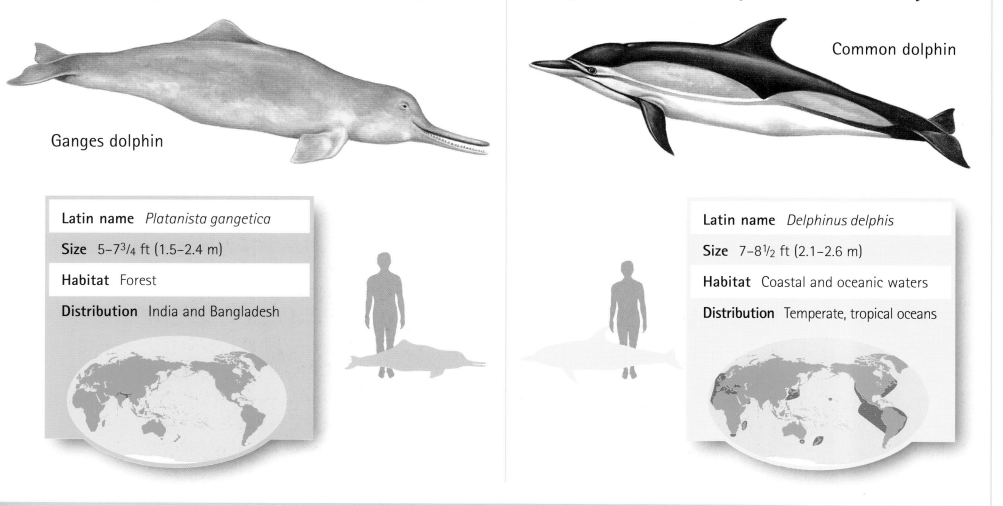

Elephants, hippos, and dugongs

African elephant

T he elephant is by far the largest land animal. There are two species, both with long, flexible, and sensitive trunks, which they use to gather food, drink, and fight. Hippopotamuses are large relatives of the pig, which spend most of their lives in water. Dugongs and manatees are completely aquatic, herbivorous mammals, with streamlined bodies, flipperlike forelimbs, and a tail.

Latin name	Loxodonta africana
Size	Body length: up to 25 ft (7.5 m)
Habitat	Forest, savanna
Distribution	Sub-Saharan Africa

Asian elephant

Asian elephant

The Asian elephant is slightly smaller than its African counterpart. It has one fingerlike extension at the end of its trunk. The main social unit is a herd led by an old female, which includes several other females, their young, and one old male. Other males may live alone, but near to the herd.

Latin name	Elephas maximus
Size	Body length: up to 21 ft (6.5 m)
Habitat	Forest, grassy plains
Distribution	India, Sri Lanka, S.E. Asia

African elephant

The African elephant has larger ears and tusks than the Asian species and two fingerlike extensions at the end of its trunk. They are social animals, and live in troops centered around several females and their young of various ages. As they mature, young males separate to form separate all-male troops.

Dugong

The dugong is a shy, solitary animal, which spends much of its time lying on the sea bed, only rising to the surface in order to breathe every couple of minutes. Seaweed and sea grass are its main food. Little is known of the dugong's reproductive habits.

Latin name	*Dugong dugon*
Size	Up to10 ft (3 m)
Habitat	Coastal waters
Distribution	Indian Ocean

Dugong

Pygmy hippopotamus

This small hippopotamus lives around swamps but spends most of its time on dry land. It has longer legs and a smaller head than its giant relative, so it is more agile on dry land. The pygmy hippo is in danger of becoming extinct because its forest habitat is being cut down. It is also at risk from hunters, who kill the animal for its meat.

Latin name	*Hippopotamus amphibius*
Size	Body length: up to 14 ft (4.2 m)
Habitat	Rivers or lakes in grassland
Distribution	Sub-Saharan Africa

Hippopotamus

Latin name	*Hexaprotodon liberiensis*
Size	Body length: up to 6¼ ft (1.9 m)
Habitat	Rain forest, swamps
Distribution	Guinea to Nigeria

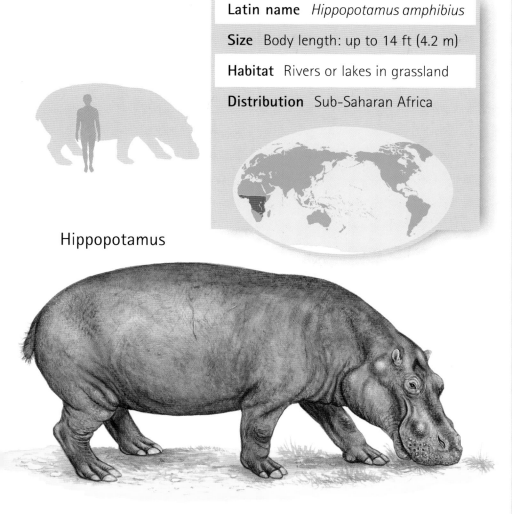

Hippopotamus

The hippo is a huge mammal that lives near rivers and lakes and spends up to 16 hours each day submerged in the water to keep cool. It emerges at sunset to graze on riverside plants and eat fallen fruit. It can swim well but often prefers to walk along the river bottom. A hippo can hold its breath underwater for up to five minutes.

Pygmy
hippopotamus

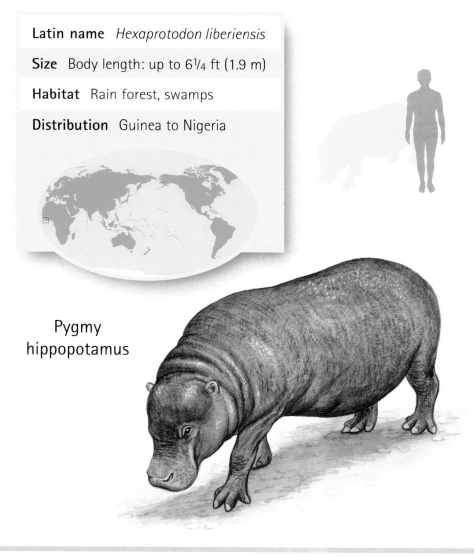

Birds

Birds are warm-blooded, air-breathing vertebrates with four limbs, one pair of which are modified to provide muscle-powered wings. All birds are feathered—a feature which no other living member of the animal kingdom shares.

Immense variety

Birds live all over the surface of Earth and inhabit almost every possible area other than the deep ocean. There are over 9,000 species of bird, ranging in size from tiny hummingbirds to the ostriches that stand taller than the average human being. While some species of bird, such as ostriches, have lost the power of flight, others, such as penguins, have adapted their wings for swimming. Others are specialized predators of the night (owls, nightjars) or of the daylight hours (eagles, hawks, falcons).

Hawk in flight

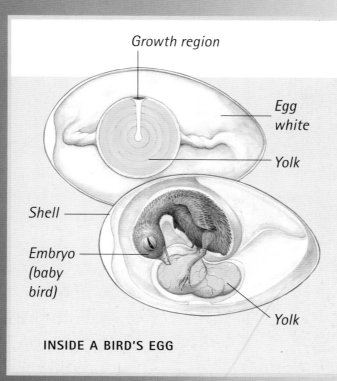

Growth region

Egg white

Yolk

Shell

Embryo (baby bird)

Yolk

INSIDE A BIRD'S EGG

Inside a bird's egg

Birds lay eggs containing large yolks, the food reserves for the developing embryo, surrounded by a tough shell. Most birds lay their eggs in a nest, where they are incubated, or kept warm, by one or both parents while the embryo develops. The young of some birds, such as ducks and peasants, hatch covered with downy feathers and are able to walk immediately. The young of others, such as most songbirds, are born naked and helpless and need a period of feeding and care from the parents.

Ratites

Ratites is the informal name given to a mixed group of running birds. Apart from the chicken sized kiwis of New Zealand, ratites are all extremely large ground-living birds, with massive, muscular legs for powerful running. Their wings are much reduced in size and cannot be used for flight. The word "ratite" means "raft-like" and refers to the shape of the breastbone found in these birds. The ratite breastbone is flat and small and has no central keel, or ridge—in other birds this keel serves for the attachment of the flight muscles.

Greater rhea

Latin name	*Rhea americana*
Size	5 ft (1.5 m) tall
Habitat	Open country
Distribution	South America

Ostrich

Ostrich

The ostrich has become so perfectly adapted to high-speed running that it is the fastest creature on two legs. At speeds of up to 44 mph (70 km/h), it can easily outstrip most enemies. Ostriches eat mostly plant food, but occasionally feed on small reptiles. Their eggs are the largest laid by any living bird.

Latin name	*Struthio camelus*
Size	6–9 ft (1.75–2.75 m) tall
Habitat	Grasslands, arid land
Distribution	Africa

Greater rhea

Greater rheas live in flocks of between 20 and 30 birds. Male and female birds look much alike. They feed on plants, seeds, insects, and some small animals. Although rheas are unable to fly, they are good swimmers and fast runners. At breeding time, males build a shallow nest and a number of females all lay their eggs in this one nest. Up to 18 eggs may be laid in a single nest.

Southern
cassowary

Latin name	*Dromaius novaehollandiae*
Size	6½ ft (2 m) tall
Habitat	Arid plains, woodland, desert
Distribution	Australia

Emu

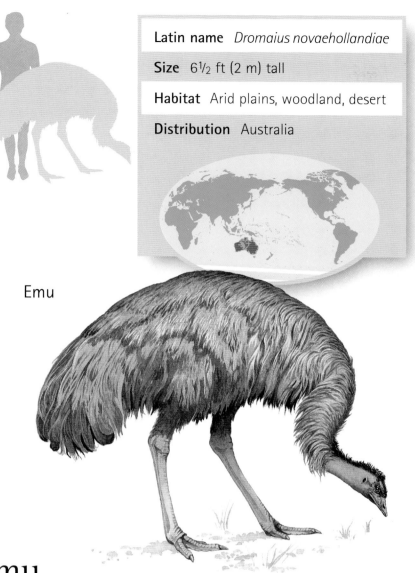

Southern cassowary

The southern cassowary is an impressive bird with long, hairlike quills that protect it from the forest undergrowth. Its legs are extremely powerful and armed with sharp-toed feet, capable of inflicting severe wounds. The head and neck are brightly colored, with wattles and a horny helmet.

Latin name	*Casuarius casuarius*
Size	5 ft (1.5 m) tall
Habitat	Rain forest
Distribution	N. Australia, New Guinea

Emu

Emus have remained common in Australia despite having been destroyed as serious pests on farmland. They can run at speeds of up to 30 mph (48 km/h) and also swim well. Fruit, berries, and insects make up the bulk of their diet. The female lays between 7 and 10 dark-green eggs in a hollow in the ground.

Latin name	*Apteryx australis*
Size	28 in (70 cm)
Habitat	Forest
Distribution	New Zealand

Kiwi

The brown kiwi is the national emblem of New Zealand. It is rarely seen and is active at night. The kiwi uses the claws on the ends of its short legs to scratch around on the forest floor in search of insects, worms, and berries. The bird's nostrils are at the tip of its pointed bill and it has a good sense of smell, which is rare among birds.

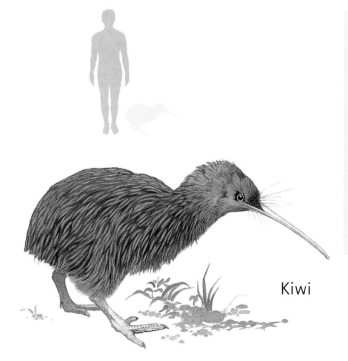

Kiwi

Taking to the air

Everything about a bird is made for flight. Much of the unique nature of a bird's body structure is linked to its need for a low take-off weight and a good power-to-weight ratio. Like mammals, birds are descended from reptilian ancestors. The heavy-boned, long, scaly body of these ancestors evolved into a lightweight, compact flying machine covered with feathers. Bird bones are slim and filled with air sacs to reduce weight, while they remain very strong. Birds' skulls are also much lighter than reptilian skulls.

Right: Kestrels are the hovering specialists of the hawk family. Even in the face of a strong gusty wind they can remain stationary in mid-air, seeking out prey.

Kestrel hovering

Long bill can push deep into a flower

Sword-billed hummingbird

Right: Hummingbirds can hover motionless in front of a flower, and fly upward, sideward, downward, and, uniquely, backward.

Power for flight

Take off and active flight require a massive output of power from the bird. The relatively huge breast muscles of a bird deliver this power to the wing bones. For these muscles to operate at the necessary high power output, good blood circulation is required and an exceptionally efficient respiratory system, to supply oxygen at the required rate. Birds have four-chambered hearts, similar to those of mammals, which can operate extremely rapidly: a sparrow's heart beats 500 times a minute, a hummingbird's up to 1,000 times a minute in flight.

Feathers for flight

Bird feathers are mostly made of a tough substance called keratin—the same substance of which reptilian scales and mammalian hairs are made. Feathers exist in a vast range of shapes, sizes, and colors, and have a variety of functions: First, they provide a light, flexible, warming protective layer over a bird's body. Second, the colors and patterns of feathers are the main way that birds communicate visually with each other. Third, the large, shaped feathers of the wings and tail provide the bird's flight surfaces. The wing feathers provide the main lift and thrust for flight, while the tail feathers help the bird steer during flight.

Bird wing shapes

The size and shape of a bird's wings indicate its habits. Some birds, such as swallows, need slender wings and forked tails for fast flying and maneuvering. Seabirds spend a lot of time gliding in the air, so their wings are long, narrow, and pointed. Falcons and other birds of prey have narrow, pointed, backward-pointing wings for high-speed flying. The wide wings of eagles and vultures, with splayed "fingers" at the tips, are for gliding at slow speeds and for soaring.

Above: Albatrosses are solidly built sea birds with long, broad wings and long legs with webbed feet. Most are white with black or gray markings. They feed along shorelines, scavenging and stealing fish from other birds.

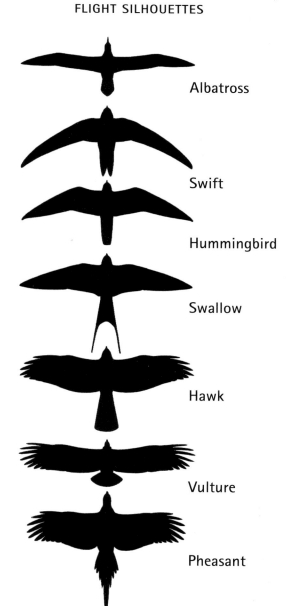

FLIGHT SILHOUETTES

Albatross

Swift

Hummingbird

Swallow

Hawk

Vulture

Pheasant

Grouse, turkeys, quails, geese, and ducks

Grouse and turkeys belong to a large and complex family of small to large game birds. The family also includes pheasants, Old World quails, and partridges. The 177 species in the family are found in habitats ranging from open to forest, from Arctic tundra to tropical forests in all continents apart from South America and Antarctica. New World quail form their own family. Geese and ducks belong to a family that also includes swans.

Latin name	*Meleagris gallopavo*
Size	35–48 in (90–122 cm)
Habitat	Wooded country
Distribution	U.S.A., Mexico

Common turkey

Black grouse

Black grouse

In spring, male grouse (called blackcocks) gather in one place. Each day at about sunrise, the males call and dance in order to attract the females. The male black grouse spreads and displays his tail. Females, or grayhens, are smaller than males and have mottled brown plumage and forked tails. Each female lays 6 to 11 eggs.

Latin name	*Tetrao tetrix*
Size	16–20 in (40–50 cm)
Habitat	Moors, forest
Distribution	N. Europe, N. Asia

Common turkey

The common turkey is a large bird with bare skin on its head and neck. Males and females look similar, but females are smaller and have duller plumage and smaller leg spurs. Turkeys are strong fliers over short distances. They roost in trees, but find most of their food on the ground—seeds, nuts, berries, insects, and small reptiles.

California quail

California quail

Latin name	*Callipepla californica*
Size	9½–11 in (24–28 cm)
Habitat	Rangeland, agricultural land
Distribution	W. U.S.A.

The state bird of California, this quail is an attractive bird with a characteristic head plume. California quails move in flocks, mostly on foot. They do not fly unless forced to do so. They feed on leaves, seeds, berries, and some insects.

Latin name	*Branta canadensis*
Size	22–43 in (56–110 cm)
Habitat	Varied
Distribution	North America, Europe, parts of Australasia

Canada goose

Mallard

The mallard is the ancestor of all domestic ducks except for muscovies. They often feed tail-up in shallow water. Female mallards have plain brownish plumage, with distinctive blue feathers on the wings. Each year, males and females bond in pairs. The female lays her 8 to 10 eggs in a nest on the ground.

Mallard

Canada goose

The 12 geographically distinct races of Canada goose live in varied habitats: from semi-desert to Arctic tundra. Races also vary greatly in size. Canada geese feed by day on grassland vegetation and aquatic plants. This migratory species uses the same routes from generation to generation and birds return to their birthplace to breed.

Latin name	*Anas platyrhynchos*
Size	16–26 in (40–65 cm)
Habitat	Almost anywhere near water
Distribution	Northern hemisphere

Nightjars, frogmouths, and owls

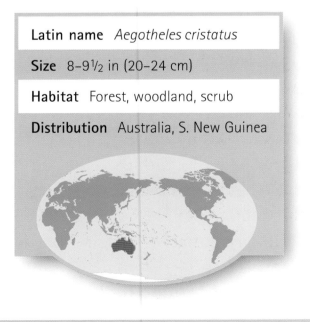

Australian owlet-nightjar

The 161 species of owl occur the world over, except on some oceanic islands. They are soft-feathered, short-tailed birds, with big heads and enormous eyes. Most owls hunt at night and feed entirely on animals from insects to birds and medium-sized mammals such as rabbits. They have exceptionally keen eyesight and excellent hearing. The frogmouths and nightjars are also night hunters. Frogmouths are tree-dwelling birds with a flat, shaggy head and large eyes. Nightjars have long, pointed wings, and large eyes for good night vision.

Australian owlet-nightjar

A shy, solitary bird, the Australian owlet-nightjar spends the day perched in an upright posture on a branch. It starts to hunt for insects and invertebrates at dusk, taking much of its prey on the ground, but also chasing aerial insects. Its bill is small and flat and is almost hidden by upward-standing bristles.

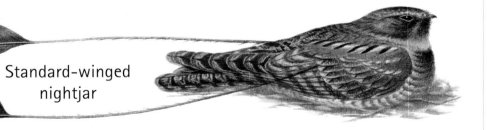

Standard-winged nightjar

Standard-winged nightjar

The standard-winged nightjar feeds on insects, which it catches in the air. In the breeding season, the male nightjar develops one elongated flight feather on each wing that grows to about 15 in (38 cm) in length. The male then flies around the female raising his elongated feathers.

Latin name	*Macrodipteryx longipennis*
Size	9 in (23 cm)
Habitat	Wooded savanna, scrub
Distribution	Africa: Chad, Sudan, Ethiopia, N. Uganda, Kenya

Latin name	*Aegotheles cristatus*
Size	8–9½ in (20–24 cm)
Habitat	Forest, woodland, scrub
Distribution	Australia, S. New Guinea

Tawny frogmouth

The tawny frogmouth hunts at night. It watches for prey, then descends silently to seize it on the ground. It eats insects, snails, frogs, and even small mammals and birds. Its nest is a flimsy platform of sticks and leaves, made on a forked branch; it may also use an old nest of another species.

Latin name	*Podargus strigoides*
Size	13–18 in (33–46 cm)
Habitat	Forest, gardens, parks
Distribution	Australia, Tasmania

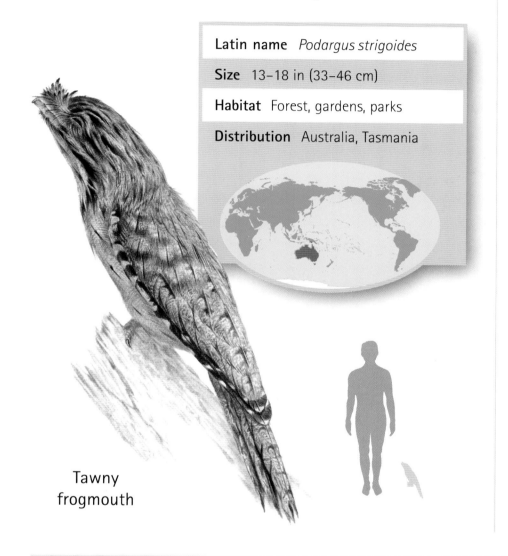

Tawny frogmouth

Latin name	*Asio otus*
Size	14–16 in (35–40 cm)
Habitat	Coniferous forest, parks
Distribution	North America, Europe, Asia

Long-eared owl

Long-eared owl

The long-eared owl has distinctive ear-tufts, which are simply feathers and have no connection with hearing. In flight, the ear-tufts are kept flat against the owl's head. It preys at night on rats, mice, shrews, moles, bats, squirrels, rabbits, and other small mammals, as well as on birds and insects. During the day it roosts in trees.

Barn owl

The barn owl is a long-legged, usually pale-plumaged bird with a white face. There are over 30 subspecies, found over a wide range. Barn owls generally live alone or in pairs and roost during the day in farm buildings, hollow trees, or caves. At night, they emerge to hunt, feeding mainly on small rodents—which they catch and kill on the ground—and also on small birds.

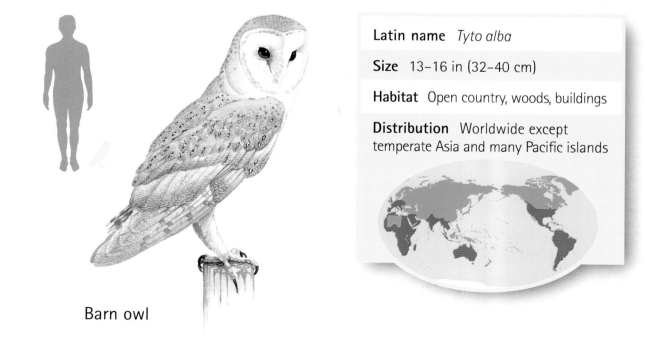

Barn owl

Latin name	*Tyto alba*
Size	13–16 in (32–40 cm)
Habitat	Open country, woods, buildings
Distribution	Worldwide except temperate Asia and many Pacific islands

Parrots and hummingbirds

The 358 species of parrot make up one of the most easily identified groups of birds. They range in size from 4 in (10 cm) to 40 in (1 m), but all species are broadly similar in appearance and structure. Most parrots are brightly colored, tree-living birds. Species include cockatoos, budgerigars, and macaws. Many parrots make loud screaming calls. Although they mimic sounds in captivity, they are not known to do so in the wild. Hummingbirds are named for the drone produced by the extremely rapid beating of their wings. They live all over the Americas, mainly in the tropics.

Sulfur-crested cockatoo

Latin name	Cacatua galerita
Size	20 in (50 cm)
Habitat	Forest, savanna, farmland
Distribution	Australasia

Budgerigar

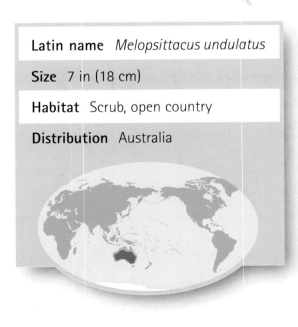

Budgerigar

The budgerigar, with its many color variations, is a popular cage bird, but in the wild its plumage is mainly green. It is active mainly in the early morning and late afternoon, when flocks of budgerigars search the ground for grass seeds, their main food. They are swift and agile in the air.

Latin name	Melopsittacus undulatus
Size	7 in (18 cm)
Habitat	Scrub, open country
Distribution	Australia

Sulfur-crested cockatoo

Sulfur-crested cockatoos are noisy, sociable birds. They move in pairs or family groups in the breeding season, but join in flocks for the rest of the year. These flocks may number hundreds of birds. Each flock leaves its roosting site at sunrise to feed on seeds, fruit, nuts, flower leaves, insects, and larvae.

Ruby-throated hummingbird

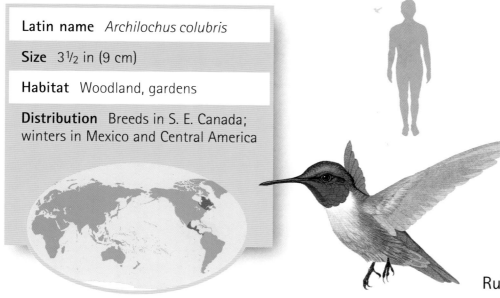

Latin name	*Archilochus colubris*
Size	3½ in (9 cm)
Habitat	Woodland, gardens
Distribution	Breeds in S. E. Canada; winters in Mexico and Central America

This tiny bird migrates 500 miles (800 km) or more across the Gulf of Mexico to its wintering grounds—an extraordinary feat for such a small animal. The male has a ruby red throat, and the female has white throat plumage and a rounded tail. The bird feeds on insects and nectar, hovering motionless in front of the flower while feeding.

Ruby-throated hummingbird

Scarlet macaw

The scarlet macaw is one of the largest and most striking parrots. Its numbers are declining because of the destruction of its rain forest habitat and the collection of large numbers of young birds for the cage-bird trade. Scarlet macaws are generally seen in pairs, family groups, or flocks of up to 20. They feed on seeds, nuts, fruit, and berries.

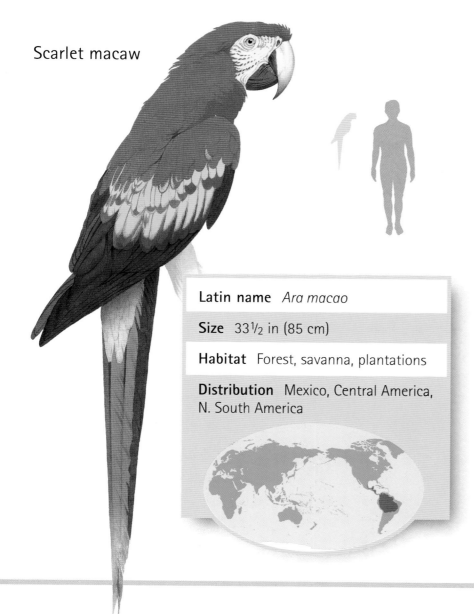

Scarlet macaw

Latin name	*Ara macao*
Size	33½ in (85 cm)
Habitat	Forest, savanna, plantations
Distribution	Mexico, Central America, N. South America

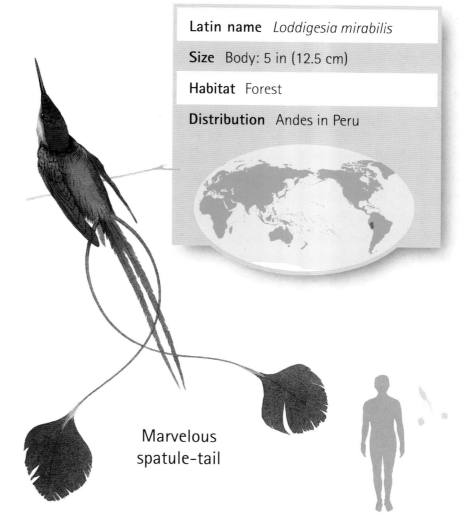

Latin name	*Loddigesia mirabilis*
Size	Body: 5 in (12.5 cm)
Habitat	Forest
Distribution	Andes in Peru

Marvelous spatule-tail

Marvelous spatule-tail

The male of this little-known hummingbird species has an extraordinary long tail with only four feathers, two of which are greatly elongated and wire-like and expanded into racquet shapes at the ends. During his courtship display, the male bird frames his iridescent throat plumage with his decorative tail feathers and flies back and forth in front of the female.

Waders

Waders are shore birds that find most of their food in water. Apart from a few species such as snipe that spend most of their time in long vegetation and are well camouflaged, most waders are found on open ground, usually on mudflats and sandy beaches. The 15 species of crane are long-legged, long-necked birds that often have brightly colored bare skin on the face and decorative plumes on the head. They are found over most of the world, except in South America, Madagascar, Malaysia, Polynesia, and New Zealand. Oystercatchers and plovers, too, are found worldwide, except on oceanic islands and in polar regions.

Black crowned crane

Latin name	*Balearica pavonina*
Size	3¼ ft (1 m) tall
Habitat	Swamps
Distribution	Central Africa

Common snipe

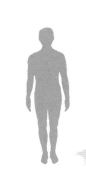

Common snipe

The common snipe is a shy bird with pointed wings, a long bill, and striped, barred plumage, which provides camouflage among vegetation. Insects are the snipe's most important food items, but it also eats earthworms, small crustaceans, snails, and plant material. Males display to females by diving through the air at great speed.

Latin name	*Gallinago gallinago*
Size	10 in (26 cm)
Habitat	Marshes, wet meadows, moors
Distribution	Breeds in Canada, N. U.S.A., Europe to N.E. Asia; winters in Central and South America, Africa, India, Indonesia

Black crowned crane

This crane's body is mostly black, and its head is topped with a crown of stiff golden feathers. Cranes perform courtship dances in the breeding season and, in a simpler form, throughout the year. The crowned crane postures with wings outstretched to display its feathers, struts about, and jumps into the air.

Common oystercatcher

The common oystercatcher has a long, blunt, flattened bill, which it uses to pry shellfish off rocks. Mollusks and crustaceans are its main food, but it also seeks insects and worms on farmland further inland. Oystercatchers are social and live in large flocks. Their nest is a hole in the ground, often lined with grass or decorated with moss.

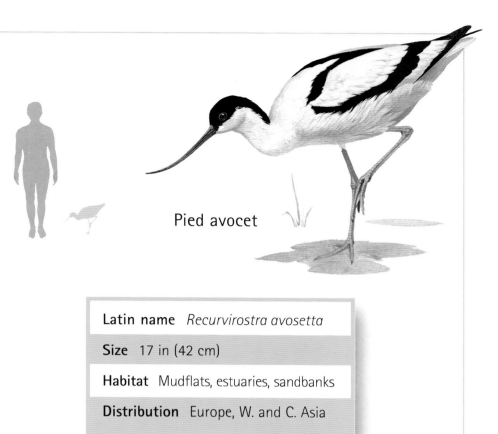

Pied avocet

Latin name	*Haematopus ostralegus*
Size	18 in (45 cm)
Habitat	Coasts, river estuaries
Distribution	Breeds Eurasia; winters S. to Africa, India, and South China

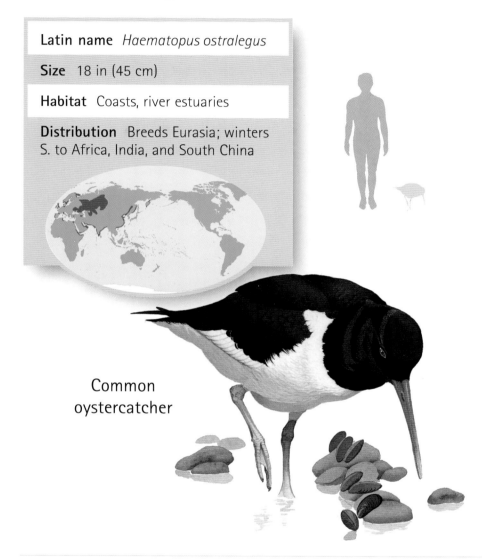

Common oystercatcher

Latin name	*Recurvirostra avosetta*
Size	17 in (42 cm)
Habitat	Mudflats, estuaries, sandbanks
Distribution	Europe, W. and C. Asia

Pied avocet

The pied avocet has striking black and white plumage and a long, upward curving bill. In flight, the long legs usually project beyond the tail. Avocets eat insects, small aquatic animals, and some plant matter, all of which they find by sweeping their bills from side to side at the surface of mud or shallow water.

American golden plover

The American golden plover flies to wintering grounds 8,000 miles (12,800 km) south of its breeding grounds on the tundra of North America and Siberia. They eat insects and some mollusks and crustaceans. Females lay 3 or 4 eggs in a shallow dip in the tundra, lined with moss and grass. Both parents incubate the eggs.

Latin name	*Pluvialis dominica*
Size	9–11 in (23–28 cm)
Habitat	Tundra, marshes, fields
Distribution	N. North America, Asia; winters in South America

American golden plover

Display and courtship

Birds signal their intent to other birds by using a series of movements or signals called a display. These may be carried out for a variety of reasons, such as when threatened or to defend territory, or for courtship. Displays also help birds identify others of their own species or identify the males in types of birds in which both sexes look alike. During the breeding season, male birds find and protect nesting sites and may sing or display to intimidate rival males and attract mates.

Left: The male blue bird of paradise hangs upside down from a branch to attract a female, its tail streamers arcing overhead.

Below: Adélie penguins dance closely and touch beaks to strengthen their bond.

Courtship displays

Courtship displays may take the form of special movements, dancing, or songs. Many species display their special plumage or brightly colored legs. Penguins choose a partner for life and, once they form a couple, they strengthen their bond by stretching their necks and calling to each other so that they recognize each other's voice. Many species dance together. They will also preen each other's feathers.

Building nests

The males of some bird species build a nest or several nests. While the male sings and displays, the female enters its territory and inspects the nest. If the female accepts the nest, she will begin to make final preparations for her clutch of eggs.

Right: A female bower bird inspects a large nest built by a male.

Displaying feathers

Peafowl are members of the pheasant family. The cock is unmistakable, with its iridsescent plumage, wiry crest, and glittering train, adorned with eye-spots. The smaller female, or peahen, has brown and some metallic green plumage and a small crest. In the breeding season, the male bird displays—fully spreading his erect train to spectacular effect by raising and spreading the tail beneath it. With his wings trailing, he prances and struts in front of the female, shivering the spread train and presenting his back view. The female may respond by a faint imitation of his posture.

Left: A peacock displays its iridescent tail feathers.

Birds of prey 1

Most birds of prey are fierce predators that are active during the day. They have keen vision, strong feet with sharp claws for seizing their prey, and a hooked beak for tearing their catch apart. The biggest family of birds of prey includes the eagles, hawks, kites, and buzzards. Eagles and buzzards generally hunt from the air, soaring over open country watching for victims. Other birds of prey, including sparrowhawks, hunt in forests and woodlands, gliding down from branches to seize prey. Vultures also belong to the eagle and hawk family, but they usually eat carrion (the bodies of dead animals).

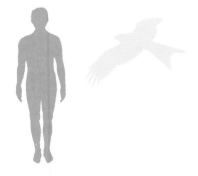

Red kite

Golden eagle

Golden eagle

Golden eagles are probably the most numerous large eagles in the world. They have huge talons with long, curved claws, a hooked bill, and exceptionally sharp-sighted eyes. While hunting, the golden eagle first soars, then dives to seize and kill the animal (usually a small mammal) with its talons.

Latin name	*Aquila chrysaetos*
Size	30–35 in (75–90 cm)
Habitat	Moor, mountain forest
Distribution	Europe, Africa north of the Sahara, N. Asia, North America

Latin name	*Milvus milvus*
Size	24–26 in (60–65 cm)
Habitat	Woodland, open country
Distribution	Europe, Middle East

Red kite

The red kite is a large bird with long wings and a deeply forked tail. It breeds in woodland but hunts in open country. As it flies low over fields, it searches for prey. It can hover briefly and pursues its prey with great agility. Small mammals up to the size of a weasel, birds, reptiles, frogs, fish, insects, and carrion are all eaten, and red kites also kill domestic poultry.

Bald eagle

The national symbol of the U.S.A., the bald eagle feeds on dead and dying fish, but it also takes live fish from the water and catches some birds and mammals. Groups of these impressive birds gather together where food is available. Bald eagles breed in northern North America on inland lakes and migrate south in the winter to find food.

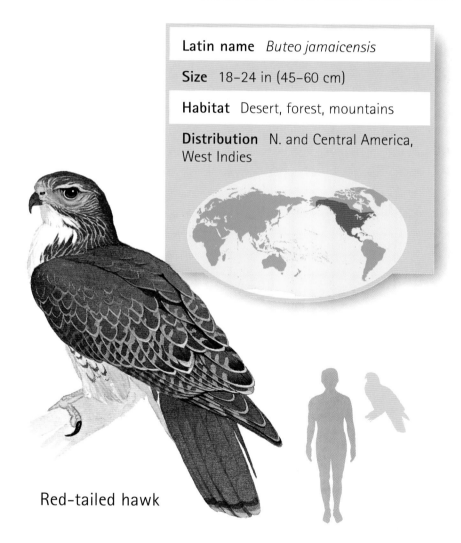

Bald eagle

Common buzzard

The buzzard eats small ground mammals, reptiles, insects, carrion, and some ground birds. It kills its prey by dropping on it from its perch or from hovering flight. Buzzards' courtship flights consist of spectacular dives and swoops. The pair will build a nest on a tree or crag, where the female lays 2 to 6 eggs.

Latin name *Buteo jamaicensis*

Size 18–24 in (45–60 cm)

Habitat Desert, forest, mountains

Distribution N. and Central America, West Indies

Latin name *Buteo buteo*

Size 20–22 in (50–55 cm)

Habitat Woodland, moorland

Distribution Europe, Asia, East Africa

Red-tailed hawk

Common buzzard

Red-tailed hawk

The red-tailed hawk is a powerful, aggressive bird with a loud voice and a distinctive chestnut tail. Its staple diet is small mammals, but it is an opportunistic hunter that also eats snakes, lizards, birds, and insects, and it can survive in a wide variety of habitats. It hunts on the wing or from a perch, swooping down on its prey.

Birds of prey 2

The falcon family includes birds such as kestrels and caracaras as well as falcons. These birds live all over the world and include the peregrine falcon—the fastest flying of all birds. Other birds of prey include the secretary bird and the osprey, both of which are the only species in their families, and the condors of South America. Like vultures, condors feed on carrion. Owls also hunt and kill prey, but they are active at night and belong in a separate group (*see* p.60).

Secretary bird

Secretary bird

The secretary bird is the only species in its family. It is an eagle-like bird with a distinctive crest, long tail feathers, and long legs. It runs to catch prey, which it takes with a swift thrust of its head; it kills larger animals by stamping on them. It lives on small mammals, insects, some birds and eggs, and reptiles.

Latin name	*Sagittarius serpentarius*
Size	5 ft (1.5 m)
Habitat	Open, grassy country
Distribution	Africa, south of the Sahara

California condor

One of the largest birds in the world, this immense vulture is also one of the heaviest of all flying birds, weighing over 25 lb (11 kg). It soars to great heights and can glide as far as 10 miles (16 km) without flapping its wings. Much of its habitat has been destroyed and it is on the verge of extinction.

Latin name	*Gymnogyps californianus*
Size	4–4½ ft (1.2–1.4 m)
Habitat	Mountains
Distribution	U.S.A.: California

California condor

Osprey

Osprey

The osprey, or fish-hawk, feeds mostly on fish, but it will sometimes take small mammals and wounded birds. When hunting, it flies over water and may hover briefly before plunging into the water, feet forward. Breeding pairs make a large nest on the ground, using sticks, seaweed, and other debris. Females lay 2 to 4 eggs, usually 3.

Latin name	*Pandion haliaetus*
Size	21–24 in (53–62 cm)
Habitat	Lakes, rivers, coasts
Distribution	Almost worldwide

Latin name	*Falco tinnunculus*
Size	13–15 in (33–38 cm)
Habitat	Open country, plains, farmland
Distribution	Europe, Asia, Africa

Common kestrel

Common kestrel

Kestrels hunt over open ground, flying some 30 to 50 ft (10 to 15 m) above ground in order to search over an area. They hover and watch, then— if prey is sighted—drop gently down on it. The diet of kestrels consists mainly of small mammals, but they will also catch small birds, reptiles, and insects. They lay clutches of 4 to 9 eggs on a ledge, in a hole in a tree, or in abandoned nests.

Peregrine falcon

The peregrine falcon is virtually without equal in the speed and precision of its flight. Birds are its chief prey. The peregrine makes a dramatic, high-speed, near-vertical dive at its prey, then kills it outright with its talons, or seizes it and takes it to the ground in order to feed. The peregrine can also chase prey through the air.

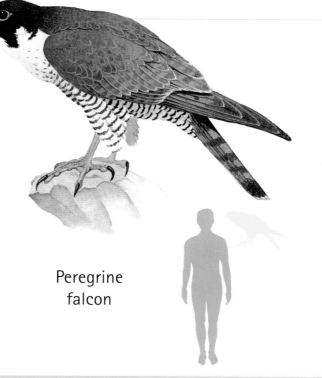

Peregrine falcon

Latin name	*Falco peregrinus*
Size	15–20 in (38–50 cm)
Habitat	Varied, mountains, cliffs
Distribution	Almost worldwide

Sparrows and finches

Sparrows are found in Africa and Eurasia to Indonesia, although some species have been introduced into other parts of the world. Sparrows roost, feed, and breed together. Most of the 36 species are ground-feeders found in open habitats, although there are some woodland species. Finches are a successful, widely distributed group of small, tree-dwelling, seed-eating songbirds. They are most numerous in Europe and northern Asia, but species occur in other parts of the Old World and in the Americas.

Northern cardinal

Latin name	Cardinalis cardinalis
Size	8–9 in (20–23 cm)
Habitat	Woodland edge, parks, gardens
Distribution	Canada, U.S.A., Mexico, Guatemala

Blue-gray tanager

Blue-gray tanager

The blue-gray tanager is at home in humid and dry areas, in coastal lowlands and up to 7,200 ft (2,200 m). They forage in pairs or in small flocks for berries, fruit, and insects, which they take from tree leaves or catch on the wing. They build cup-shaped nests and the female lays 2 or 3 eggs.

Latin name	Thraupis episcopus
Size	6½ in (16 cm)
Habitat	Woodland, parks, gardens
Distribution	S.E. Mexico, Central and South America to Brazil and Bolivia

Northern cardinal

The male cardinal is an unmistakable, brilliant-red bird, while the female is buffy-brown, with a reddish tinge on its wings and crest and a red bill. They are aggressive birds with a varied range of songs. They feed on the ground and in trees on seeds and berries and, in the breeding season, also take insects.

Chipping sparrow

Male and female chipping sparrows have chestnut caps, edged by white eyebrow stripes. They are inconspicuous birds and often live in suburban and inhabited areas. Grass seeds are their main food, but they also eat weed seeds, insects, and spiders. The female bird makes a nest in a vine, tree, or bush, and lays 3 to 5 eggs.

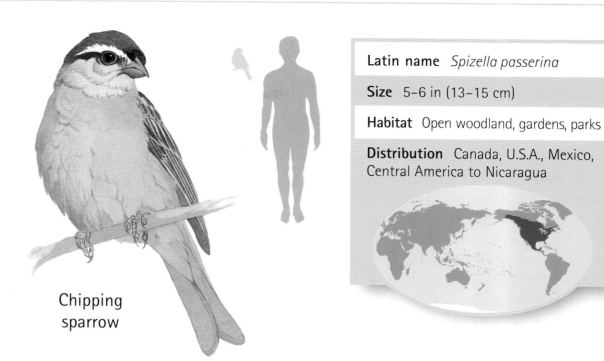

Chipping sparrow

Latin name	*Spizella passerina*
Size	5–6 in (13–15 cm)
Habitat	Open woodland, gardens, parks
Distribution	Canada, U.S.A., Mexico, Central America to Nicaragua

Latin name	*Ramphocelus carbo*
Size	7 in (18 cm)
Habitat	Woodland, cultivated land
Distribution	N. South America, south to Bolivia, Paraguay, Brazil

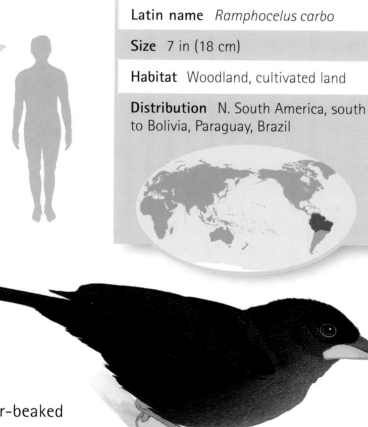

Silver-beaked tanager

Purple honeycreeper

Purple honeycreepers live in wooded areas. Fruit, especially bananas, and insects are important foods, but these birds also perch by flowers and suck nectar from them with their long, curved bills. The male bird is largely bluish-purple and black, with yellow legs, while the female is green, with buff and blue patches on the head and breast.

Latin name	*Cyanerpes caeruleus*
Size	4 in (10 cm)
Habitat	Forests of all types
Distribution	N. South America to Bolivia, Paraguay, Brazil

Silver-beaked tanager

The silver-beaked tanager has a silvery-white base to the lower part of its black beak. The plumage of male birds varies slightly from area to area, ranging from black to dark maroon on the upper parts, with a red throat and breast. They live on or near the edge of wooded areas, where they forage for insects and fruit from low tree branches.

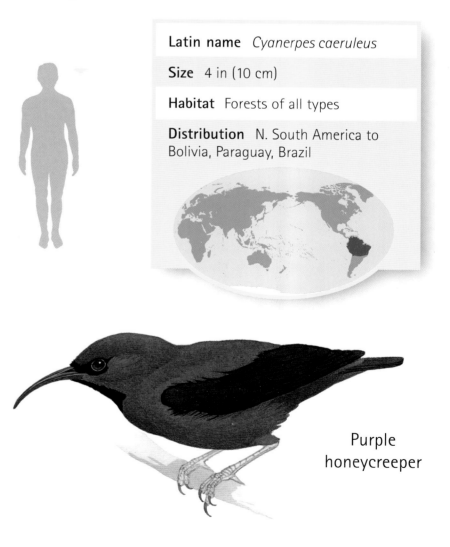

Purple honeycreeper

Reptiles

Reptiles are air-breathing vertebrates that include alligators and crocodiles, lizards, snakes, and turtles, as well as extinct related forms such as dinosaurs. Reptiles are cold-blooded animals—they cannot regulate their own body temperatures—and most lay eggs.

Tyrannosaurus

Prehistoric reptiles

The first reptiles appeared some 300 million years ago. They evolved from amphibians and may have looked similar to some modern-day lizards. About 230 to 70 million years ago, flying reptiles, or pterosaurs, appeared and dominated the air for over 100 million years, while dinosaurs, such as the mighty *Tyrannosaurus rex*, ruled the land and reptiles called ichthyosaurs and plesiosaurs lived in the seas. Reptiles laid eggs with hard shells that did not need water—unlike amphibian eggs—allowing reptiles to inhabit a greater range of habitats. Early reptiles also produced the ancestors of the remaining two groups of land-based vertebrates: the mammals and the birds.

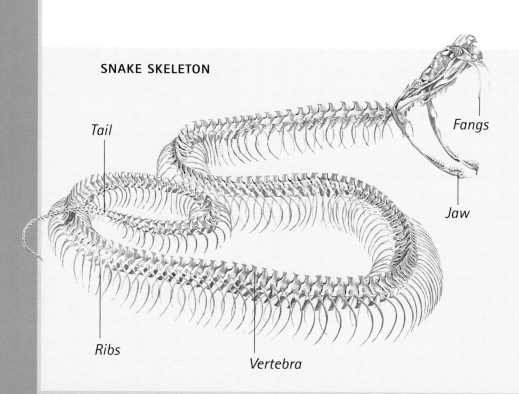

SNAKE SKELETON

Tail

Fangs

Jaw

Ribs

Vertebra

Reptile skeletons

Reptiles are vertebrates (they have backbones). When they are born, they look like smaller versions of the adults. Reptile skeletons vary from the specialized forms of lizards, which adapted for life in a variety of habitats including trees and bushes, to turtles, which, uniquely among modern-day reptiles, have developed an armored shell. Snakes have very strong, flexible backbones—the longer snakes have as many as 400 vertebrae along their backbones.

Turtles and tortoises

Turtles and tortoises belong to the order chelonia. There are about 230 living species. A typical chelonid has its short, broad body enclosed in a shell made of two layers: an outer layer of horny shields and an inner layer of bone. The ribs and most of the vertebrae are attached to the shell. The long neck can usually be withdrawn into the shell. Chelonids have no teeth, but their jaws have horny beaks of varying strength. All lay eggs, usually burying them in sand or earth. Hatchlings must dig their way out to the surface.

Galápagos giant tortoise

Latin name	Geochelone nigra
Size	Up to 4 ft (1.2 m)
Habitat	Moist forest to arid land
Distribution	Galápagos Islands

Spur-thighed tortoise

Spur-thighed tortoise

These tortoises hibernate in winter. They court in spring, the male butting and biting the female before mating with her. The eggs, usually two or three in a clutch, are laid in May and June and generally hatch in September or October. The young tortoises are similar to adults, with more rounded shells and clearer markings.

Latin name	Testudo graeca
Size	6 in (15 cm)
Habitat	Meadows, cultivated land, wood
Distribution	N. Africa; extreme S.E. and S.W. Europe; Middle East

Galápagos giant tortoise

At least 13 subspecies of these tortoises live on the Galápagos Islands. Because the populations are isolated from one another on different islands, over thousands of years subspecies have evolved, varying in size, length and thickness of limbs, and shape of shell. The tortoises eat almost any vegetation. Males are markedly larger than females.

Hawksbill turtle

The hawksbill's beautiful shell is the reason for the endangered status of this species. The turtle uses its pointed head to search out mollusks and crustaceans in rocky crevices and reefs. They lay more eggs at a time than any other turtle, usually a batch of about 150.

Latin name	*Eretmochelys imbricata*
Size	30–36 in (75–90 cm)
Habitat	Coral reefs, rocky coasts
Distribution	Tropical Atlantic, Pacific and Indian Oceans; Caribbean

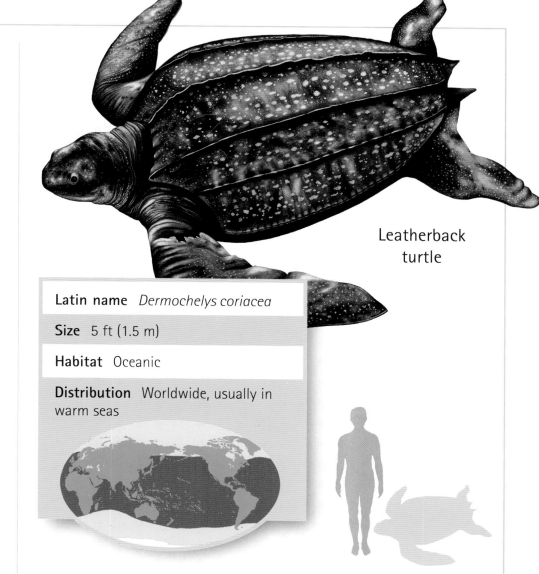

Leatherback turtle

Latin name	*Dermochelys coriacea*
Size	5 ft (1.5 m)
Habitat	Oceanic
Distribution	Worldwide, usually in warm seas

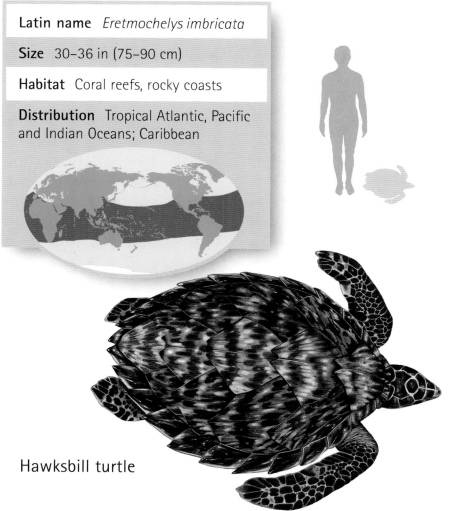

Hawksbill turtle

Leatherback

The leatherback is the world's largest turtle. Its flippers are extremely long, with a span of about 9 ft (2.7 m). Its shell resembles hard rubber. The turtle feeds mainly on jellyfish using its weak, scissorlike jaws. They migrate long distances between nesting and feeding sites.

Yellow mud turtle

The yellow mud turtle seems to prefer water with a mud bottom, but it may also be found in artificial habitats such as cattle drinking troughs and ditches. The turtle feeds on both aquatic and terrestrial invertebrates. It gives off a musky odor from two pairs of glands, positioned on each side of the body where skin and shell meet. Breeding females lay two to four eggs.

Latin name	*Kinosternon flavescens*
Size	3½–6 in (9–15 cm)
Habitat	Slow streams
Distribution	U.S.A.: Nebraska to Texas; Mexico

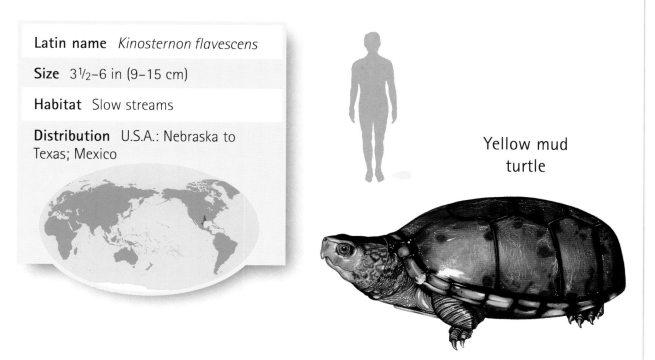

Yellow mud turtle

Eggs, nests, and young reptiles

Reptiles are usually born on land and develop inside an egg. Some lizards and snakes, however, give birth to fully developed young. The eggs of most reptiles have a soft and flexible shell, although some have hard shells like birds' eggs. The young reptile inside the egg is cushioned in a bag of fluid called the amnion. The reptile absorbs oxygen and moisture through the shell, while the yolk provides it with food.

Below: Newly hatched turtles move as fast as they can from their nesting site on the sand to the relative safety of the sea.

Young reptiles

Whether they are born from eggs or are born live, young reptiles are able to feed themselves and live in much the same habitat as they live in as adults. Unlike most amphibians, young reptiles do not pass through a larval or tadpole stageduring which they look completely different from their parents. They are not dependent on their parents to feed them and care for them, as most mammals and birds are. Reptiles usually start off eating small prey and move on to increasingly large prey as they grow bigger.

Baby turtles

Nile crocodile

Babies in mother's mouth

Left: The Nile crocodile mother carries her newly hatched young inside her mouth from the nest to a safe nursery area, where she cares for them for three to six months.

Turtles

Turtles gather in large numbers in order to travel to certain suitable nesting areas. The females lay their eggs on sandbanks that are exposed only in the dry season, and there are relatively few such sites. The females come out on to the sandbanks at night and each lays her eggs. They then return to their feeding grounds. When the hatchlings emerge from their shells, they are in immediate danger from predators, so must head straight for the sea.

Turtle nest sites

A female turtle usually makes her nest at the top of a beach. She digs an egg cavity using her cupped rear flippers as shovels. The egg cavity is shaped roughly like a tear drop and is usually tilted slightly. She then lays her eggs, usually two or three at a time. The average size of a clutch ranges from about 80 to 120 eggs, depending on the species. Because the eggs are flexible, they do not break as they fall into the chamber. After laying her eggs, the turtle covers the nest with sand and scatters sand over the top for camouflage. She then returns to the sea.

Eggs

FEMALE TURTLE LAYING EGGS IN SAND

Right: Sea turtles come ashore at night to lay their eggs. They usually return to the same beach on which they were born, using the Earth's magnetic field to help them navigate.

Lizards

There are over 3,000 species of lizard. They live in many different habitats, including in trees, on the ground, and in water. Examples of lizards include iguanas and chameleons. The iguana family includes more than 600 species, the vast majority living in the Americas, although a few species live in Madagascar and Fiji. Most iguanas are ground- or tree-living and feed on insects and small invertebrates. Many are brightly colored and perform elaborate courtship rituals. About 85 species of chameleons are known, most of them living in Africa and Madagascar.

Common iguana

Latin name	*Iguana iguana*
Size	3¼–6½ ft (1–2 m)
Habitat	Forest, trees near water
Distribution	Central and N. South America; introduced into U.S.A.: Florida

Marine iguana

Marine iguana

The marine iguana is the only present-day lizard to use the sea as a major habitat. It forages for seaweed, its main food. When swimming, the iguana uses its powerful tail for propulsion; its feet are usually held against its body, but they are sometimes used to steer a course.
The iguana cannot breathe underwater.

Latin name	*Amblyrhynchus cristatus*
Size	4–5 ft (1.2–1.5 m) long
Habitat	Lava rocks on coasts
Distribution	Galápagos Islands

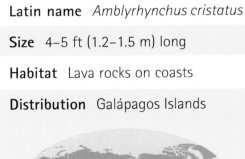

Common iguana

The common iguana has a crest of comb-like spines running all the way down its body and tail. The bands across the shoulders and tail become darker as the iguana gets older—young iguanas are bright green. Active by day, these iguanas are agile tree-dwelling lizards that feed on plants. They can defend themselves with their teeth and claws if attacked. Females lay around 40 eggs.

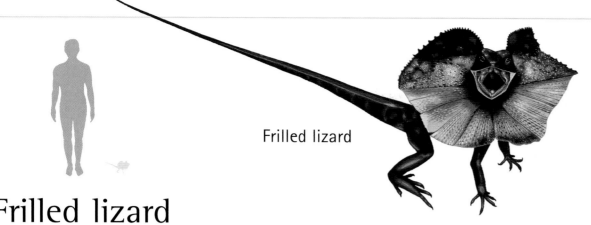

Frilled lizard

Latin name *Chlamydosaurus kingii*

Size 26 in (66 cm) including tail

Habitat Dry forest, woodland

Distribution Australia: N. Western Australia, N. Northern Territory, E. Queensland; New Guinea

Frilled lizard

This slender, long-tailed lizard has an extraordinary collar of skin around its neck. Normally this collar lies in folds around the neck and shoulders, but if alarmed, the lizard opens its mouth wide and opens its frill, making the animal look larger than it really is.

Latin name *Chamaeleo jacksonii*

Size 4¼–4¾ in (11–12 cm)

Habitat Savanna vegetation

Distribution E. Africa: Uganda, Tanzania to N. Mozambique

Desert night lizard

The desert night lizard varies in coloration over its range but is marked with many small dark spots. It lives on yucca plants and agaves and feeds on termites, ants, beetles, and flies, which it finds among vegetation or rocks. Night lizards give birth to live young, which are born tail first.

Jackson's chameleon

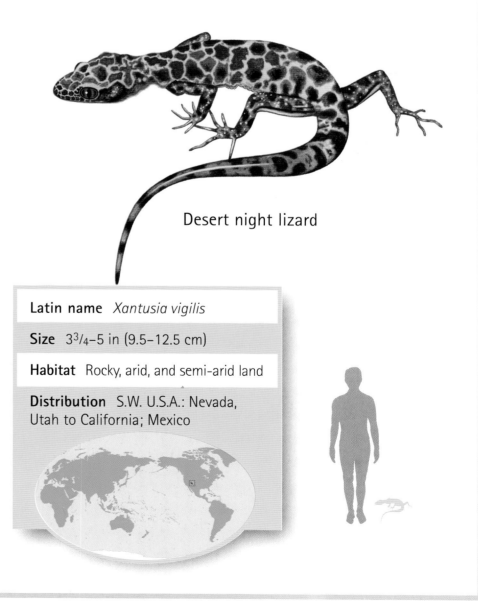

Desert night lizard

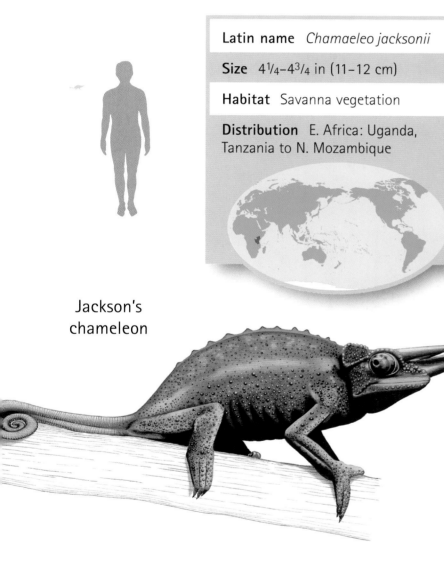

Jackson's chameleon

The three horns on his head make the male Jackson's chameleon instantly recognizable. The female has only one horn on the snout and smaller horns by each eye. Usually colored a dull green, this chameleon resembles lichen on the bark of a tree. Like all chameleons, it has skin that changes color to reflect its emotional state.

Latin name *Xantusia vigilis*

Size 3¾–5 in (9.5–12.5 cm)

Habitat Rocky, arid, and semi-arid land

Distribution S.W. U.S.A.: Nevada, Utah to California; Mexico

Snakes

Snakes probably evolved from burrowing lizards that lost their legs as they adapted to life below ground. Despite being legless, snakes are very mobile and can move over every type of terrain. A snake grips the ground with its scaly skin and pushes itself along using muscles attached to its ribs. The four main types of motion are called serpentine, concertina, sidewinding, and linear. Snakes are also expert climbers and swimmers. Some can even glide through the air. A snake must shed its skin regularly to allow for growth. It rubs its snout on a rough surface to loosen the skin and then wriggles out of it, revealing a new layer of scales beneath. This is called sloughing.

Latin name *Naja naja*

Size 6–7¼ ft (1.8–2.2 m)

Habitat Rainforest, cultivated land

Distribution India, central and southeastern Asia, Philippines

Indian cobra

Common garter snake

Latin name *Thamnophis sirtalis*

Size 18 in–4¼ ft (45 cm–1.3 m)

Habitat Fields, woodland

Distribution South Canada, U.S.A.

Common garter snake

The common garter snake likes moist places and is often found in wet meadows, beside streams, and in drainage ditches. It slithers through damp vegetation searching for prey such as salamanders, frogs, toads, and earthworms. The female garter snake gives birth to as many as 50 live young.

Indian cobra

This large, very poisonous cobra feeds on mice, lizards, and frogs. Its poison can cause severe pain if it reaches the eyes of mammals. To threaten enemies, the cobra raises the front of its body and spreads the ribs and loose skin at its neck to form a hood shape. Eye-like markings on the hood confuse the enemy further. Cobras adapt well to life in cities, feeding on the rodents in sewers.

Eastern coral snake

The colorful markings of the coral snake are a warning to enemies that it is highly poisonous. This snake spends much of its time buried in sand or dead leaves. In the morning and late afternoon, it moves around searching for small snakes and lizards, which it kills with its poisonous bite.

Latin name	*Micrurus fulvius*
Size	22–48 in (55–120 cm)
Habitat	Forest and rocky hillsides
Distribution	S. E. U.S.A., N.E. Mexico

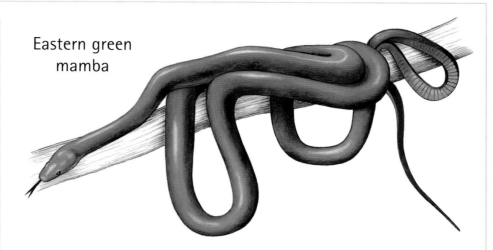

Eastern green mamba

Eastern green mamba

The slender, fast-moving mambas spend much of their lives in trees, where they feed on birds and lizards. Their venom is extremely toxic, but these snakes are not generally aggressive unless provoked and tend rather to flee from danger or threat.

Latin name	*Dendroaspis angusticeps*
Size	6½ ft (2 m)
Habitat	Savanna
Distribution	E. and S. Africa

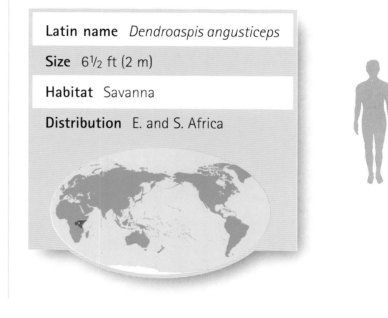

Eastern coral snake

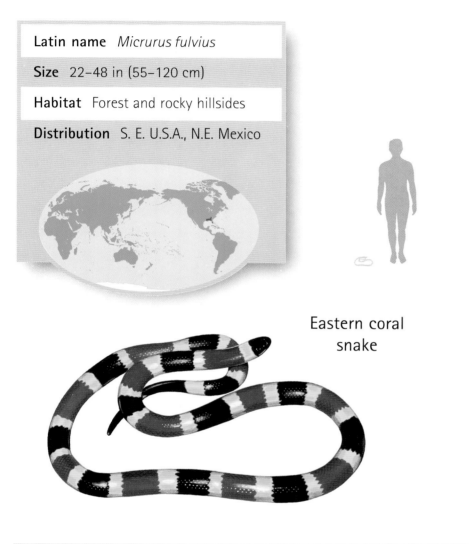

Latin name	*Dipsas indica*
Size	About 27 in (68 cm)
Habitat	Forest
Distribution	Tropical South America

Snail-eating snake

The snail-eating snake is a nocturnal, ground-dwelling species. Its upper jaw is short with few teeth, and its lower jaw long with elongated, curved teeth. The structure of the jaws is such that the lower jaw can be swung backward and forward without moving the upper jaw. This arrangement is ideal for crushing the shells of snails.

Snail-eating snake

Vipers

The viperidae family has two subfamilies: Viperinae (true vipers) and Crotalinae (pit vipers). There are about 50 species of viper, found all over the Old World except in Australia and Madagascar. Vipers ambush and strike their prey with their large fangs. Pit vipers are also highly venomous. They occur in eastern Europe, in the Americas, and throughout mainland Asia and Japan. Pit vipers possess sensory pits on each side of the head that can detect heat and which are used at night to locate warmblooded prey. The viper kills with a rapid strike, using its long, curved fangs.

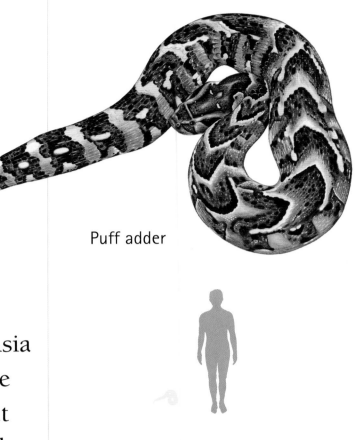

Puff adder

Latin name *Bitis arietans*

Size 3½–4½ ft (1.1–1.4 m) long

Habitat Mountain slopes, forest

Distribution Africa: Morocco, S. of the Sahara to South Africa; Middle East

Fer-de-lance

Fer-de-lance

The fer-de-lance is a common pit viper whose color and pattern vary over its range. A sheath of flesh covers its fangs, but when the snake bites the sheath is pushed back. The fer-de-lance feeds mainly on small mammals and its venom causes rapid and severe internal bleeding. The female gives birth to up to 50 live young in a yearly litter—a large number for a pit viper.

Latin name *Bothrops atrox*

Size 8 ft (2.45 m)

Habitat Low coastal areas

Distribution S. Mexico to South America; West Indies

Puff adder

Perhaps the most common and widespread African snake, the puff adder adapts to both moist and arid climates, but not to the extremes of desert or rainforest. It is one of the biggest vipers and can inflate its body even more when about to strike. Its fangs are about ½ in (1.25 cm) long. This ground-living snake feeds on rats, mice, birds, lizards, frogs, and toads.

Desert
sidewinding viper

Latin name *Vipera peringueyi*

Size 10 in (25 cm)

Habitat Desert

Distribution Africa: Namibia

Desert sidewinding viper

This small, rare viper species is found on the coastal sand-dunes of the Namib Desert in Africa. It glides over the dunes with a side-winding motion. During the day it half-buries itself in the sand—a feat it can accomplish in about 20 seconds—to shelter from the sun or to lie in wait for prey such as rodents or lizards.

Sidewinder

The sidewinder is a small, agile snake with a horn-like projection over each eye. It hides during the day. At night it emerges to hunt its prey, mainly small rodents and lizards. This desert snake moves with a sideways motion, known as sidewinding, thought to be the most efficient mode of movement for a snake on sand.

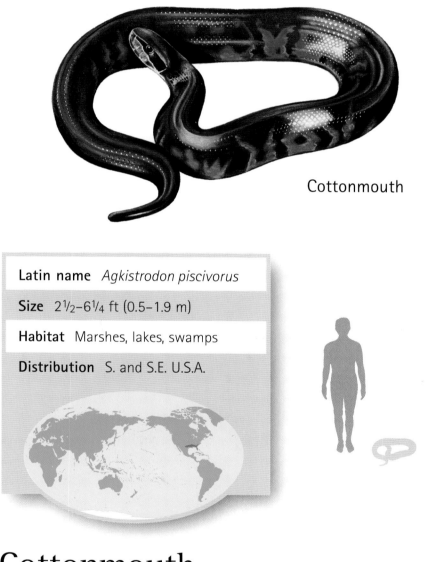

Cottonmouth

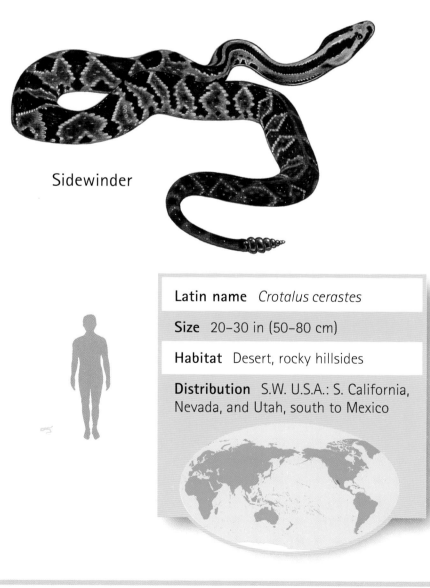

Sidewinder

Latin name *Agkistrodon piscivorus*

Size 2½–6¼ ft (0.5–1.9 m)

Habitat Marshes, lakes, swamps

Distribution S. and S.E. U.S.A.

Latin name *Crotalus cerastes*

Size 20–30 in (50–80 cm)

Habitat Desert, rocky hillsides

Distribution S.W. U.S.A.: S. California, Nevada, and Utah, south to Mexico

Cottonmouth

This heavy-bodied cottonmouth spends much of its life either in or near water. It swims well, holding its head up out of the water. This snake is most active at night, when it preys on amphibians, fish, snakes, and birds, and is one of the few snakes to eat carrion. Its venom is extremely dangerous. Female cottonmouths breed every other year.

Geckos, monitors, and gila monster

Komodo dragon

Some 700 species of gecko are found in tropical, subtropical, and warm temperate zones. They live in forests, swamps, deserts, and mountainous areas. Geckos have a flattened head and soft, scaly skin. Most have enormous eyes. Many have "friction pads" under their toes, which enable them to climb up vertical surfaces and even to walk upside down. Monitor lizards are found in Africa, Asia, and Australia. They have long necks and well-developed limbs. Their tongues are forked, like a snake's. The gila monster is related to monitor lizards.

Latin name	*Varanus komodensis*
Size	10 ft (3 m)
Habitat	Grassland
Distribution	Islands of Komodo, Flores, Pintja, and Padar, east of Java

Nile monitor

Nile monitor

This strong reptile swims and dives well, using its tail as a rudder. It can also climb trees, using its strong tail to hold onto branches. It has huge claws, which it uses to dig burrows. Nile monitors stay near water, feeding on frogs, fish, and snails, as well as crocodile eggs and young.

Latin name	*Varanus niloticus*
Size	Over 6½ ft (2 m)
Habitat	Forest, open country
Distribution	Africa: south and east of the Sahara to Cape Province

Komodo dragon

The awe-inspiring Komodo dragon dwarfs most present-day lizards. It has a heavy body, a long tail, and large limbs with claws. Its teeth are large and jagged and its tongue is forked. It is a good climber and swims well. It preys on animals as large as hog deer and wild boar, as well as small deer and pigs.

Leaf-tailed gecko

This gecko's mottled body blends well with bark or lichen. It lies with its body pressed against a branch or trunk of a tree. It can also change the intensity of its coloration, becoming darker by night and lighter again in the morning. When alarmed, it turns dark brown or black. It can use its flat tail to hold on to branches. This lizard feeds on insects.

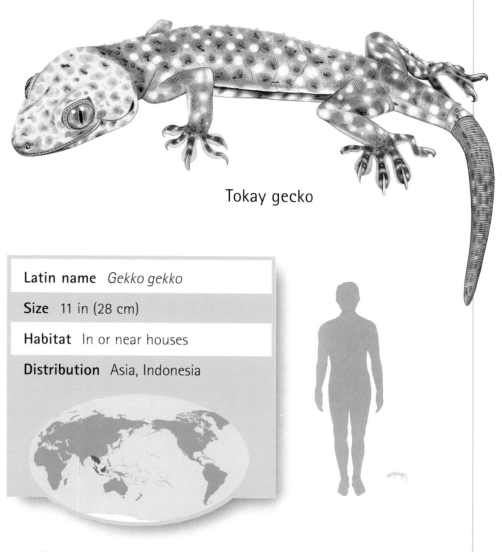

Tokay gecko

Latin name	*Uroplatus fimbriatus*
Size	8 in (20.5 cm)
Habitat	Forest
Distribution	Madagascar

Latin name	*Gekko gekko*
Size	11 in (28 cm)
Habitat	In or near houses
Distribution	Asia, Indonesia

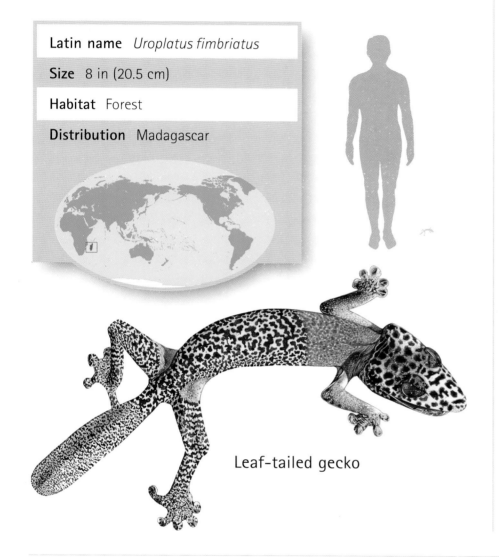

Leaf-tailed gecko

Tokay gecko

This is one of the largest and most common geckos. It is believed to bring good luck to the houses in which it lives. It eats insects, particularly cockroaches, and young lizards, mice, and small birds, all of which it seizes in its powerful jaws, The male makes his loud barking call, "tokeh" or "gekoh," most frequently in the mating season.

Latin name	*Heloderma suspectum*
Size	18–24 in (45–60 cm)
Habitat	Arid and semiarid areas
Distribution	S.W. U.S.A.: S. Utah, Arizona to New Mexico; Mexico

Gila monster

Gila monster

The venomous gila monster is a heavy-bodied lizard with a short, usually stout tail, in which it stores fat. It can then live off these fat reserves during periods of food shortage. It is brightly colored with bead-like scales on its back. The gila lives on the ground and takes shelter under rocks or in a burrow. It hunts mostly at night.

Venomous reptiles

Snakes are the only poisonous, or venomous, reptiles, apart from two species of lizard. Poisonous snakes exist worldwide but the most venomous species are found in tropical areas. Snakes inject poison, or venom, into prey using specially adapted teeth or fangs. Mostly, these fangs are positioned at the front of the upper jaw, as in vipers and cobras, but in some species they are located at the back. Venom stuns the prey so the snake can then kill it. Sometimes, it is used for defense.

Right: The cobra rears up in attack position. Its open hood enhances the imposing effect.

Top of the windpipe extends to front of the mouth so cobra can breathe while swallowing prey

Attack position

The fangs of most venomous snakes fold away in the mouth when they are not needed. When the snake opens its mouth to strike, the fangs flick forward. The cobra's open hood is a warning signal to deter other animals from attacking it. Most snakes wil try to avoid a fight, escaping where possible.

Cobra

Left: All 50 or so species of sea snakes are venomous. Some are known to have venom 10 times as strong as rattlesnake venom, making them the most poisonous snakes in the world.

Venomous lizards

The only venomous lizards are the two members of the gila monster family: the gila monster, from western North America, and the Mexican beaded lizard. Their venom is produced in glands in the lower jaw and enters the mouth via grooved teeth at the front of the lower jaw. The poison, diluted in saliva, flows into the victim as the lizard chews. The Gila monster's bite is normally not fatal to humans, but it can bite quickly and holds on with great strength.

Gila monster

Above: The venomous gila monster is a formidable looking, heavy-bodied lizard with brightly colored bead-like scales on its back.

Types of snake fang

Most venomous snakes' fangs are hollow and deliver the liquid poison under pressure like a syringe. The fangs are either long and folded back against the roof of the mouth until they are needed, or shorter but fixed in the jaw. Snake venom is a highly modified saliva that is produced by special glands usually situated on each side of the head below and behind the eye. The venom is then stored in special sacs before it is forced through the hollow fangs. In some snakes, the venom fangs are grooved rather than hollow. Most snakes deliver venom by biting, but some snakes, such as spitting cobras, shoot venom from the mouth.

FANG POSITIONS

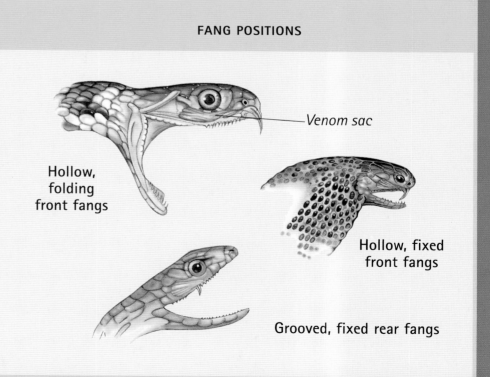

Venom sac

Hollow, folding front fangs

Hollow, fixed front fangs

Grooved, fixed rear fangs

Crocodiles, alligators, and caimans

Estuarine crocodile

The order Crocodilia is made up of crocodiles, alligators, caimans, and the single species of gharial. All are powerful amphibious carnivores that prey on a range of vertebrate animals, although young crocodiles also eat insects and other small invertebrates. Crocodiles are archosaurs, the group of reptiles that includes the dinosaur, which were the dominant animal life forms from 190 to 65 million years ago. Their bodies are covered with horny scales, while bony plates on the back give added protection.

Latin name	*Crocodylus niloticus*
Size	15–20 ft (4.5–6 m)
Habitat	Large rivers, lakes, marshes
Distribution	Africa (not Sahara or N.W.)

Latin name	*Crocodylus porosus*
Size	8–23 ft (2.5–7 m)
Habitat	Estuaries, coasts, mangroves
Distribution	S. India through Indonesia; N. Australia

Nile crocodile

Nile crocodile

This crocodile preys on mammals and birds that come to the water's edge to drink. After seizing its catch, the crocodile drowns it by holding it under the water, before twisting off chunks of flesh by spinning its own body in the water while holding onto the prey. It does not need to feed every day.

Estuarine crocodile

The estuarine crocodile is one of the largest and most dangerous species and has been known to attack man. Its hide is considered the most valuable of all crocodiles for leather, and, despite restrictions on hunting, it is rapidly being exterminated. It spends little time on land and swims great distances. The female lays 25 to 90 eggs.

Spectacled caiman

Latin name	*Caiman crocodilus*
Size	5–6½ ft (1.5–2 m)
Habitat	Slow waters, lakes, swamps
Distribution	Venezuela to S. Amazon basin

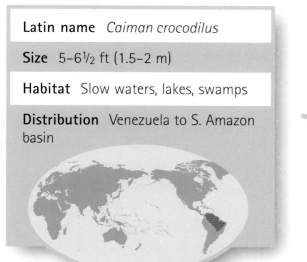

The common name of this caiman comes from the ridge on the head between the eyes which resembles the bridge of a pair of spectacles. The population of wild caimans has declined drastically because they are hunted not only for skins, but the young are also collected and sold as pets or stuffed.

Spectacled caiman

Indian gharial

The Indian gharial has an extremely long, narrow snout, studded with about 100 small teeth—ideal for seizing fish and frogs underwater. Like all crocodiles, the gharial has been hunted for its skin and it is now extremely rare. Its hind legs are paddle-like and the gharial rarely leaves the water except to nest.

Latin name	*Gavialis gangeticus*
Size	Up to 19½ ft (6 m)
Habitat	Large rivers
Distribution	N. India

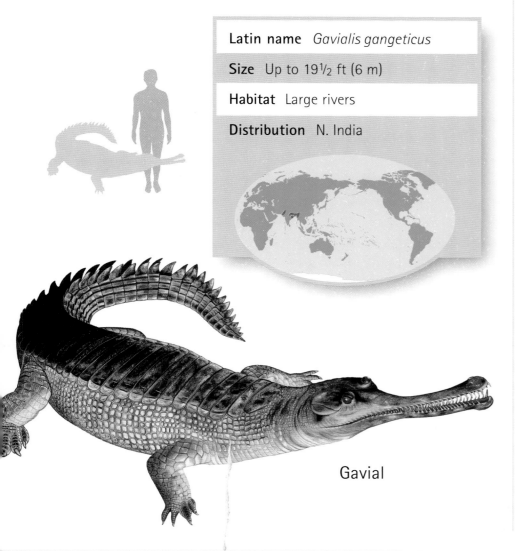

Gavial

Latin name	*Alligator mississipiensis*
Size	Up to 18 ft (5.5 m)
Habitat	Marshes, rivers, swamps
Distribution	S.E. U.S.A.

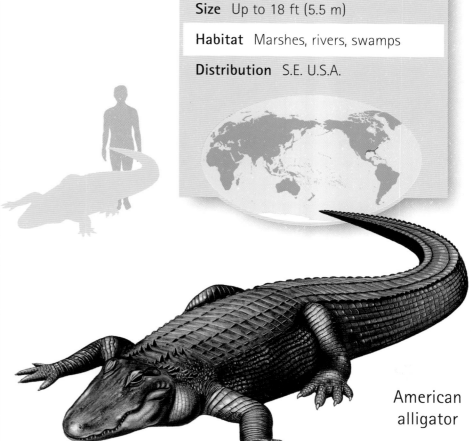

American alligator

American alligator

The American alligator once struggled for survival against hunters and habitat destruction. It has now been protected by conservation laws and the population is on the increase. These alligators mate in shallow water in April. The male stays with the female for several days before mating, stroking her body with his forelimbs.

Amphibians

Amphibians are cold-blooded vertebrates. They cannot control their own body temperature, so some bask in the sun to warm up and enter water to cool down. Although most have lungs, amphibians gain much of the oxygen they need through their skin.

Amphibian skeletons

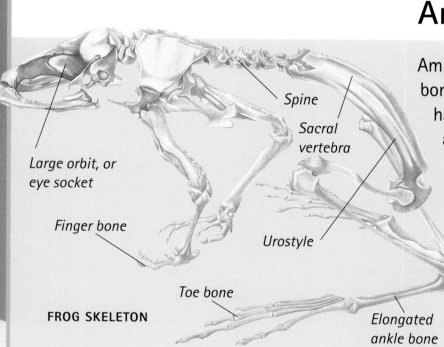

Large orbit, or eye socket

Finger bone

Spine

Sacral vertebra

Urostyle

Toe bone

Elongated ankle bone

FROG SKELETON

Amphibians have simple skeletons, with fewer bones than other modern vertebrates. Frogs have broad heads with large eye sockets and a short spine (usually with no ribs). The tail bones have fused into a rod-like bone called the urostyle, while a single sacral vertebra (backbone) forms the hump in sitting frogs. The leg, feet, and toe bones are long, and the elongated ankle bones enable the legs to fold for jumping. Adaptations to this form allow frogs to live in different habitats.

Kinds of amphibians

The three groups of amphibians are salamanders and newts, frogs and toads, and caecilians. A typical salamander has a long body and tail and four legs. Although similar to a lizard in shape, it does not have scaly skin or ear openings on the outside of its body. Frogs and toads have much shorter bodies than salamanders and no tails. Their well-developed back legs are used for jumping on land and swimming in water. Caecilians are wormlike and live in burrows. They are rarely seen above ground.

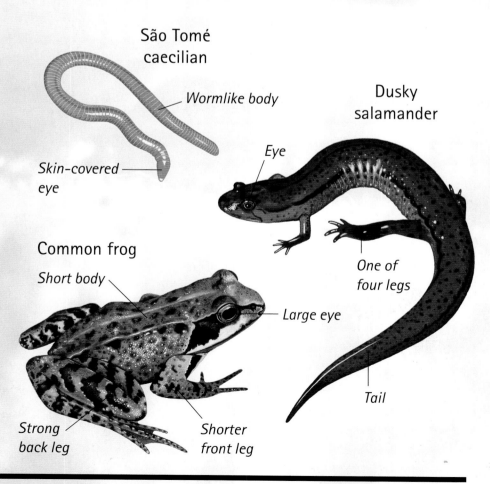

São Tomé caecilian

Wormlike body

Skin-covered eye

Dusky salamander

Eye

One of four legs

Tail

Common frog

Short body

Large eye

Strong back leg

Shorter front leg

Frogs and toads 1

Oriental
fire-bellied
toad

There are more than 3,500 species of frog and toad and all are very similar in appearance, whatever their lifestyle. They live all over the world, except in Antarctica. A typical frog or toad has long back legs, webbed toes, and no tail. The skin may be smooth or warty but is always moist. Like all amphibians, frogs and toads are at home both on land and in fresh water and can swim, hop, and even climb trees. Most feed on small creatures such as slugs, snails, and insects, which they catch with their long sticky tongue.

Latin name	*Bombina orientalis*
Size	2 in (5 cm)
Habitat	Mountain streams, rice fields
Distribution	Siberia, N.E. China, Korea

Common toad

Common toad

The common toad is the largest European toad, and females are generally larger than males. This heavily built toad has extremely warty skin. It hides during the day, often using the same spot time after time, and emerges at dusk to feed on a variety of insects, spiders, and worms. The toad usually moves by walking but, if distressed, may hop.

Latin name	*Bufo bufo*
Size	Up to 6 in (15 cm)
Habitat	Varied, often fairly dry
Distribution	Europe, N. Africa, N. Asia to Japan

Oriental fire-bellied toad

A brilliantly colored species, the oriental fire-bellied toad's rough skin exudes a milky secretion that is extremely irritating to the mouths and eyes of potential predators. Unlike most frogs, its disk-shaped tongue cannot be flipped forward to capture prey. The female lays her eggs on the underside of submerged stones in small clumps, each containing between 2 and 8 eggs.

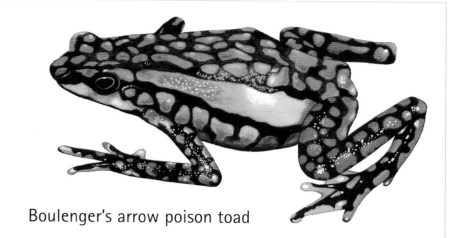

Boulenger's arrow poison toad

Latin name	*Pipa pipa*
Size	5–8 in (12.5–20 cm)
Habitat	Streams, rivers
Distribution	N. South America

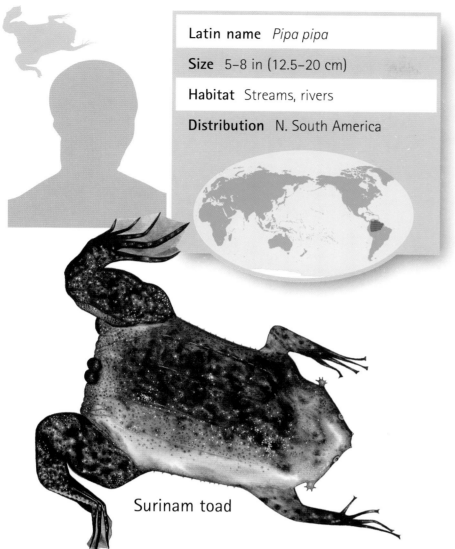

Surinam toad

Boulenger's arrow poison toad

The black and orange markings of Boulenger's arrow poison toad warn of the poisonous skin that defends it from predators. This rare species is active during the day and may climb up into bushes at night. Its tadpoles probably have sucking mouths to anchor themselves to rocks on the riverbed.

Latin name	*Atelopus boulengeri*
Size	About 1 in (2.5 cm)
Habitat	Forested slopes of the Andes
Distribution	South America: Ecuador, Peru

Surinam toad

This active, strong-swimming toad will eat almost anything it can find, even carrion. It uses its slender fingers to forage for food items. During the Surinam toad's extraordinary mating ritual, the male and female somersault through the water until between 40 and 100 eggs have been laid.

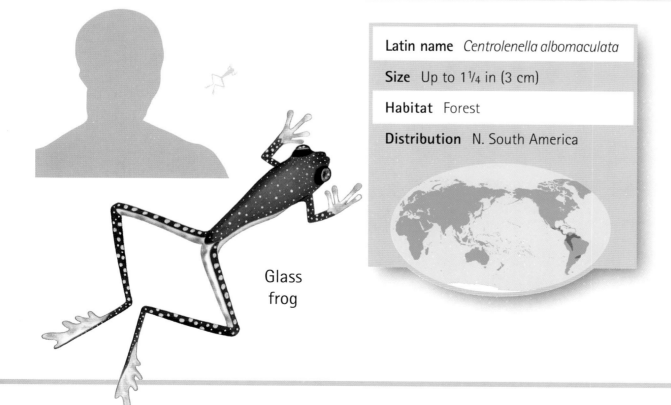

Glass frog

Latin name	*Centrolenella albomaculata*
Size	Up to 1¼ in (3 cm)
Habitat	Forest
Distribution	N. South America

Glass frog

The glass frog is so called because its lightly colored skin allows the internal organs to be seen. It lives in small trees and bushes, usually near to running water. Its fingers are expanded into disks that give a good grip when it is climbing. It lays its eggs in clusters on the underside of leaves overhanging running water. When the tadpoles hatch, they tumble down into the water.

Frogs and toads 2

Wallace's flying frog

Frogs and toads usually breed in water. They lay eggs, which hatch into tailed young called tadpoles. The tadpoles live in water, breathing through feathery gills and eating plants. As they grow they lose their gills and tail and develop legs and lungs. They grow into tiny versions of their parents, able to breathe air and hop around on land. Some of the most specialized frogs are the tree frogs, which have special pads on their feet to help them climb and run around in trees.

Latin name	*Rhacophorus nigropalmatus*
Size	4 in (10 cm)
Habitat	Rain forest
Distribution	S.E. Asia

Common frog

Common frog

European frogs are divided into two groups—green and brown frogs. The brown frogs, of which the common frog is an example, tend to be more territorial and have quieter voices than the green frogs. The common frog varies in color from brown or gray to yellow. Much of its life is spent on land; it enters water mainly to mate or hibernate.

Latin name	*Rana temporaria*
Size	Up to 4 in (10 cm)
Habitat	Any moist area near water
Distribution	Europe, east to Asia

Wallace's flying frog

This frog glides from tree to tree in the forest. It has a distinctive broad head and a long, slim body. The feet are greatly enlarged and fully webbed, and the tips of the fingers expand into large disks. Flaps of skin fringe the forelimbs and heels. It can launch itself into the air and glide gently down to another branch or to the ground.

Lutz's
phrynomedusa

Latin name	*Phyllomedusa appendiculata*
Size	1½ in (4 cm)
Habitat	Forest, near moving water
Distribution	South America: S.E. Brazil

Lutz's phrynomedusa

A tree-dwelling frog, Lutz's phrynomedusa has triangular flaps of skin on each heel, which may help it to camouflage its outline. Areas of red skin can be flashed to confuse predators. It eats mainly insects. Its eggs are laid onto a folded-over leaf overhanging water.

Latin name	*Hyperolius horstockii*
Size	Up to 2¼ in (6 cm)
Habitat	Swamps, dams, streams, rivers
Distribution	South Africa

Horned frog

The horned frog is almost as broad as it is long and has a wide, powerful head and large mouth. Its eyes are small, with a small bulge on each upper eyelid. Its toes are partially webbed, although the frog spends much of its life half-buried in the ground. Snails, small frogs, and rodents are all eaten, and it is also believed to eat the young of its own species.

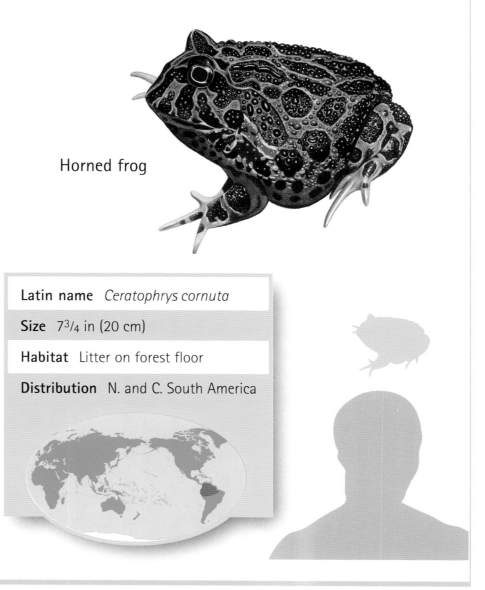

Horned frog

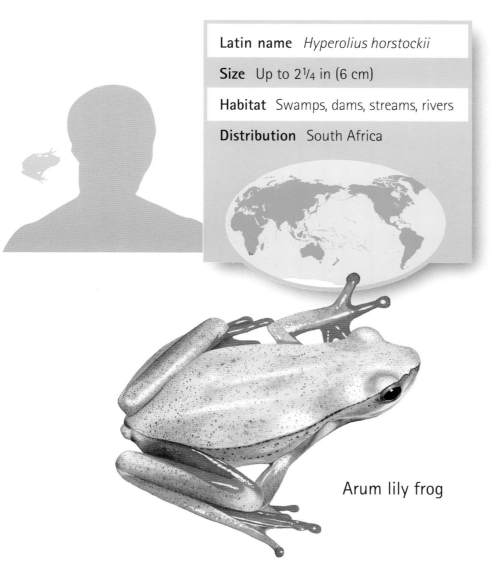

Arum lily frog

Arum lily frog

The long-limbed arum lily frog is a good climber. Its feet are equipped with expanded, adhesive disks and are only partially webbed. The under-surfaces of the limbs are orange. The rest of the body changes color to help the frog control its body heat, becoming a light cream in bright sun and dark brown in shade.

Latin name	*Ceratophrys cornuta*
Size	7¾ in (20 cm)
Habitat	Litter on forest floor
Distribution	N. and C. South America

Amphibian metamorphosis

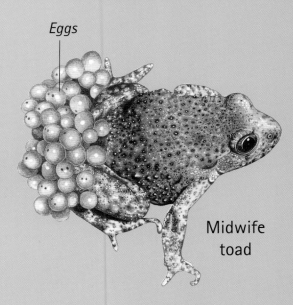

Eggs

Midwife toad

Amphibians lay eggs, which hatch into larvae (immature forms). In frogs and toads, larvae are called tadpoles and they look quite different from adults. The process of changing into the adult form is called metamorphosis. It takes about 12 to 16 weeks for frog or toad tadpoles to develop into froglets (miniature frogs with tails, which are eventually absorbed by the body). Newts, salamanders, and caecilians also undergo a metamorphosis, but the change in body shape is less obvious.

Above: The male midwife toad from Western Europe twists strings of between 35 and 50 eggs around his legs. He carries the eggs in this way while they develop, taking care that they do not dry out by moisturizing them in pools.

Right: At this stage in the tadpole's development, it is half-tadpole, half-frog.

Tadpole

Developing tadpole

From about six weeks, tadpoles begin to look more like adult frogs, with hind legs, a longer body, and a more-defined head. The hind legs help the tail to propel the tadpole through the water. The front legs will develop from the bulge on either side of the top of the body.

Hind leg

Life cycle of a frog

Frogs typically lay eggs in water. A tadpole emerges from each egg and swims freely within the water. Tadpoles have gills, a tail, and a small circular mouth—but no legs. Metamorphosis begins with the development of the hind legs, then the front legs. The lungs develop, and the tadpole begins to swim to the surface of the water to breathe. The intestine shortens to allow a carnivorous diet, and the eyes begin to project from the top of the head. In frogs, the tail is absorbed by the body for the last stage of metamorphosis.

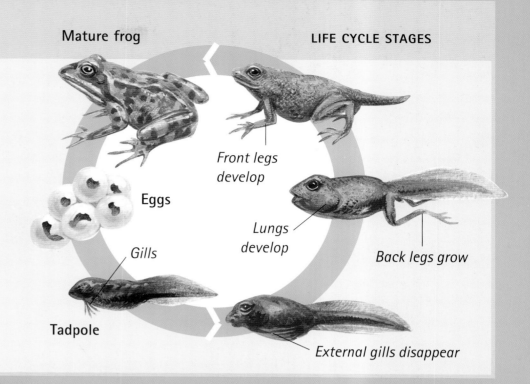

Mature frog

LIFE CYCLE STAGES

Front legs develop

Eggs

Lungs develop

Back legs grow

Gills

Tadpole

External gills disappear

Variations

Not all amphibians lay eggs in water, leaving them to hatch into freely swimming tadpoles. Some lay their eggs in a sheltered spot, often on land, while others carry the eggs around on their backs, or in a skin pocket. Some species store the eggs inside their bodies, either in their vocal sac or in their stomach. Metamorphosis can take place within an egg, which then hatches into a small adult.

Left: The common frog breeds in spring. The females lay clusters of up to 4,000 eggs in shallow ponds. Each egg develops into a tadpole, but just one or two of these will survive into adulthood.

Salamanders

Salamanders are lizard-like tailed amphibians with soft, moist, scaleless skin. The most successful group of living salamanders is the lungless salamander family, with over 200 of the 350 or so known salamanders. As their name suggests, these salamanders have a total absence of lungs. The animal obtains oxygen instead through its moist skin or through the internal surface of the mouth cavity. Nearly all lungless salamanders live in North or South America. The smaller family of mole salamanders has 32 species, all found in North America from Canada to Mexico. These salamanders have broad heads and a thick-bodied, sturdy appearance.

Tiger salamander

This species is the world's largest land-dwelling salamander. It has a stout body, broad head, and small eyes. Its coloration varies greatly, and it adapts to a variety of habitats from sea level up to 11,000 ft (3,400 m). It lives near water among plant debris or shelters in the burrows of crayfish or mammals. It is active at night and feeds on worms, insects, mice, and amphibians.

Texas blind salamander

Texas blind salamander

This rare species is a typical cave dweller, with its ghostly pale body and tiny eyes. Its external gills are red and feathery and it has long, thin legs. The Texas blind salamander eats cave-dwelling invertebrates that feed on the droppings left by the bats that roost in the caves.

Latin name	*Eurycea rathbuni*
Size	3½–5¼ in (9–13.5 cm)
Habitat	Underground waters
Distribution	U.S.A.: extreme S. Texas

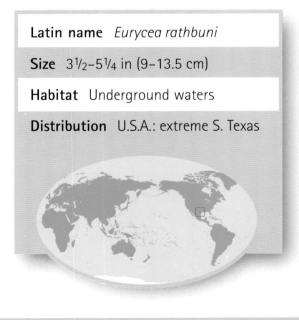

Latin name	*Ambystoma tigrinum*
Size	6–15¾ in (15–40 cm)
Habitat	Plains, damp meadows, forest
Distribution	S.C. Canada, C. U.S.A., south to N. Florida and Mexico

Red salamander

A brilliantly colored species, the red salamander has a stout body and short tail and legs. It spends much of its life on land but is usually close to water. Earthworms, insects, and small salamanders are its main food. The female red salamander lays a clutch of between 50 and 100 eggs in the fall.

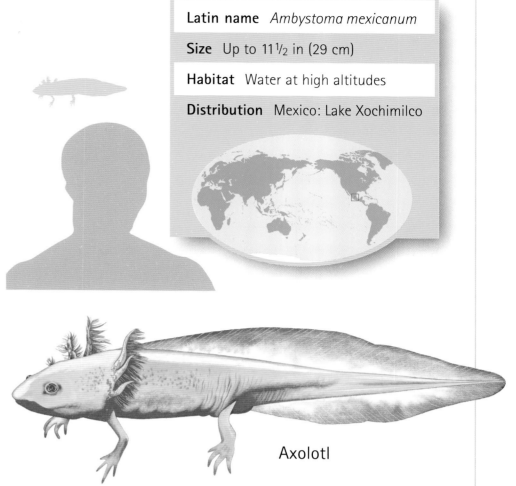

Latin name	*Ambystoma mexicanum*
Size	Up to 11½ in (29 cm)
Habitat	Water at high altitudes
Distribution	Mexico: Lake Xochimilco

Latin name	*Pseudotriton ruber*
Size	3¾–7 in (9.5–18 cm)
Habitat	Springs, woodland, swamps
Distribution	E. U.S.A.: S. New York, west to Indiana, south to Louisiana

Axolotl

Red salamander

Axolotl

Now rare, the axolotl is threatened by the destruction of its habitat. It can spend its entire life in a larval form, even breeding in this state, but it may mature into a salamander if the pond in which it lives dries out. The word "axolotl" is an Aztec word meaning water monster. Axolotls breed in water, laying about 400 eggs in the wild.

Spotted salamander

This stout-bodied salamander is identified by the irregular spots on its back, which run from head to tail. Rarely seen, it spends most of its life underground and feeds on slugs and worms. In some areas these salamanders are becoming rare because acid rain is polluting their breeding pools and preventing the successful development of eggs.

Latin name	*Ambystoma maculatum*
Size	6–9½ in (15–24 cm)
Habitat	Forest, hillsides near water
Distribution	S.E. Canada, E. U.S.A. to Georgia and E. Texas

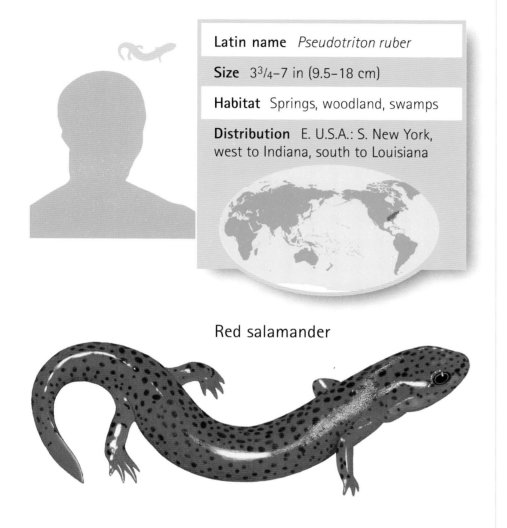

Spotted salamander

Newts and caecilians

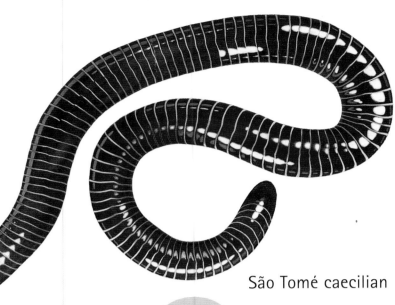

São Tomé caecilian

Newts are a type of salamander. They have well-developed limbs with four or five digits and movable eyelids; adults have fully functional lungs and no external gills. There are both aquatic and terrestrial forms, but most are found in or near water, at least in the breeding season. Caecilians are limbless amphibians with cylindrical, ringed bodies, like giant earthworms. One family is aquatic, but the others are blind, burrowing creatures, rarely seen above ground.

Latin name	*Schistometopum thomensis*
Size	Up to 12 in (30 cm)
Habitat	Forest
Distribution	São Tomé Island off W. Africa

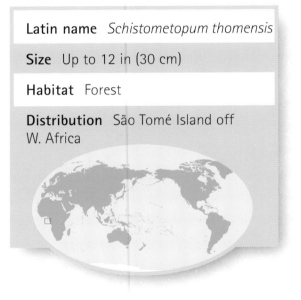

Sticky caecilian

Sticky caecilian

Adult caecilians of this Southeast Asian genus live in burrows and feed on earthworms and small burrowing snakes. They breed in the spring. The female lays 20 or more eggs in a burrow she makes in moist ground near to water. She coils around her eggs, which absorb moisture and gradually swell to double their original size.

Latin name	*Ichthyophis glutinosus*
Size	Up to 15 in (38 cm)
Habitat	Forest
Distribution	S.E. Asia

São Tomé caecilian

The body of this brightly colored caecilian is usually about ½ in (1.25 cm) in diameter. Its snout is rounded and it has no tail. It lives underground, feeding on whatever invertebrate prey it can find, mainly insects and worms. The female retains her eggs in her body while they develop and hatch; the young are then born well developed.

Eastern newt

The eastern newt occurs in several different patterns and colors over its wide range. Adults are aquatic and are eager predators, searching in shallow water for worms, insects, crustaceans, and the eggs and young of other amphibians. The female lays from 200 to 400 eggs, one at a time, on underwater plants.

Latin name *Notophthalmus viridescens*

Size 2½–5½ in (6.5–14 cm)

Habitat Ponds, lakes, ditches, swamps

Distribution S.E. Canada, E. U.S.A.

Eastern newt

Warty/great crested newt

A large, rough-skinned newt, the male warty newt develops a jagged crest on his back in the breeding season. Females are often larger than males, but do not develop crests. Warty newts eat invertebrates. They will also take some small fish and other amphibians and their eggs. The female lays 200–300 eggs, which hatch after 2 or 3 weeks.

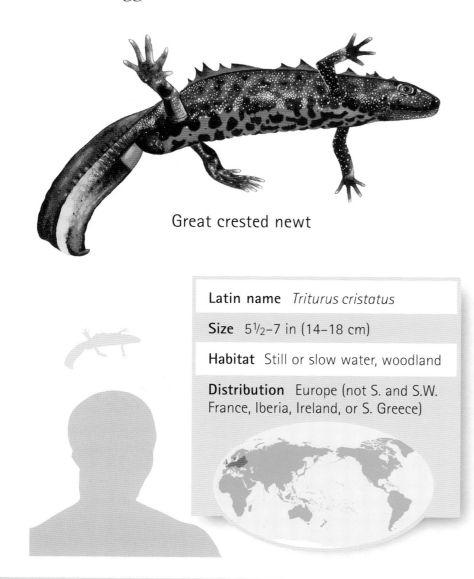

Great crested newt

Latin name *Triturus cristatus*

Size 5½–7 in (14–18 cm)

Habitat Still or slow water, woodland

Distribution Europe (not S. and S.W. France, Iberia, Ireland, or S. Greece)

Latin name *Cryptobranchus alleganiensis*

Size 12–30 in (30–75 cm)

Habitat Rocky-bottomed streams

Distribution E. U.S.A.: S. New York to N. Alabama, Missouri

Hellbender

Hellbender

Despite its name, this giant salamander is a harmless creature that feeds on crayfish, snails, and worms. Like newts, the hellbender has fully developed lungs. It is nocturnal, and depends on its sense of smell and touch, rather than on sight, to find its prey. Hellbenders breed in the fall, when the female lays 200 to 500 eggs.

Fish

Fish are aquatic vertebrates that are typically cold-blooded, covered with scales, and equipped with two sets of paired fins and several unpaired fins. More than 45,000 known species of fish live in the sea and in fresh water, from surface level to the ocean depths.

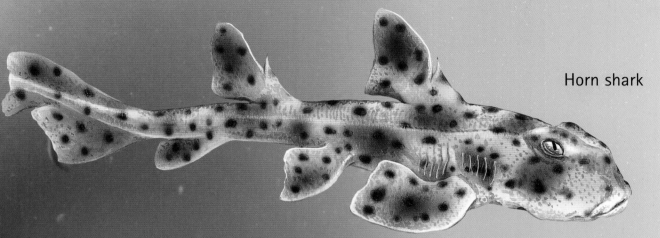

Horn shark

Types of fish

Fish have evolved into a huge range of specialized forms. The first major division is between jawless and jawed fish. Jawless fish today consist of only lampreys and hagfish, remnants of an earlier stage of vertebrate development. The jawed fish, which first appeared just under 400 million years ago, are divided into different groups. First are the fish with skeletons made of a tough, elastic tissue called cartilage. These include sharks, skates, and rays. Second, there are the bony-skeletoned fish, of which there are 24,000 or so species—about half the known total of living fish species.

Fish skeletons

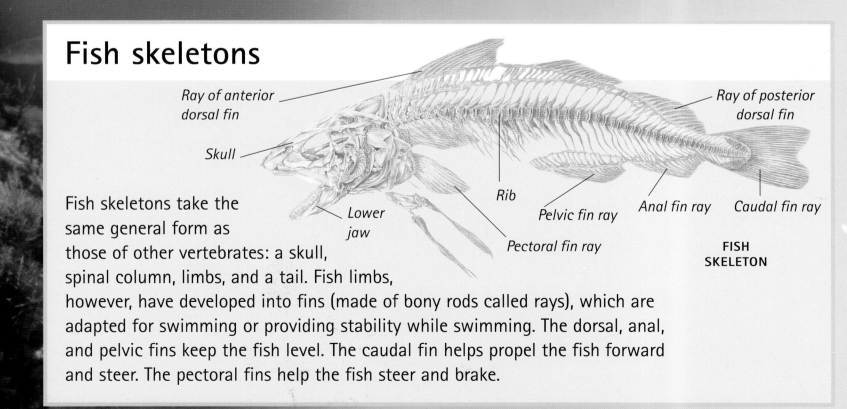

Ray of anterior dorsal fin

Ray of posterior dorsal fin

Skull

Rib

Lower jaw

Pelvic fin ray

Anal fin ray

Caudal fin ray

Pectoral fin ray

FISH SKELETON

Fish skeletons take the same general form as those of other vertebrates: a skull, spinal column, limbs, and a tail. Fish limbs, however, have developed into fins (made of bony rods called rays), which are adapted for swimming or providing stability while swimming. The dorsal, anal, and pelvic fins keep the fish level. The caudal fin helps propel the fish forward and steer. The pectoral fins help the fish steer and brake.

Sharks

White shark

There are about 375 species of shark, ranging in size from the smallest at about 12 in (30 cm) in length to the whale shark at more than 50 ft (15 m) long. About half of all shark species, however, are less than 3¼ ft (1 m) long. Sharks are cartilaginous fish, which means they have skeletons made of flexible, gristlelike cartilage rather than bone. They have a streamlined, torpedo-shaped body, five to seven gill openings on each side of the head, and tough skin covered with small toothlike scales. Most sharks live in the sea, although a few live in or enter inland waters. Sharks feed on fish and other creatures.

Latin name	*Carcharodon carcharias*
Size	Up to 20 ft (6 m)
Habitat	Open sea; coastal waters
Distribution	Atlantic, Pacific, and Indian Oceans

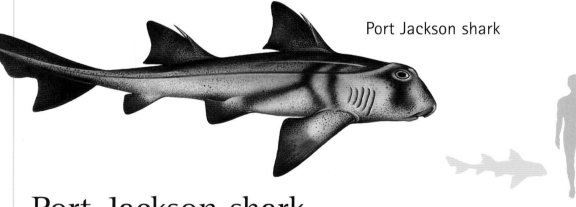

Port Jackson shark

Port Jackson shark

The Port Jackson shark has the large, heavy head, prominent forehead, and ridge over each eye that are typical of all bullhead sharks. The shark's small mouth has sharp, pointed teeth at the front and broader, crushing teeth farther back, probably for crushing the shells of mollusks and crustaceans. Most feeding takes place at night.

Latin name	*Heterodontus portusjacksoni*
Size	Up to 5 ft (1.5 m)
Habitat	Coastal waters
Distribution	S. Pacific Ocean, Southern Ocean: coasts of Australia

White shark

The white shark, also known as the great white shark, is not actually white, but ranges in color from gray to brown with white underparts. Its long snout is pointed, and its large, powerful teeth are triangular and serrated. It feeds on many kinds of aquatic animal, such as fish (including other sharks), seals, and dolphins, and it also scavenges on dead animals.

Thresher shark

Latin name	*Alopias vulpinus*
Size	Up to 20 ft (6 m)
Habitat	Surface waters in open sea
Distribution	Temperate and tropical oceans

The distinctive thresher shark has a tail as long as the rest of its body, which it uses when hunting. The sharks feed mainly on schooling fish and, working in pairs or alone, they lash their tails to herd the fish into a compact group where they make easy prey. A thresher may also strike and stun an individual fish with its tail.

Thresher shark

Smooth hammerhead

This is one of 10 species of hammerhead sharks, all of which have flattened projections at the sides of the head. The eyes are on the outer edges of these lobes, and the nostrils are also spread far apart. The smooth hammerhead feeds on fish, particularly rays, and also scavenges. They are aggressive sharks and have been known to attack humans.

Latin name	*Cetorhinus maximus*
Size	Up to 34 ft (10.4 m)
Habitat	Oceanic
Distribution	Worldwide, outside the tropics

Basking shark

Latin name	*Sphyrna zygaena*
Size	Up to 14 ft (4.3 m)
Habitat	Coastal and inshore waters
Distribution	Atlantic, Pacific, and Indian Oceans

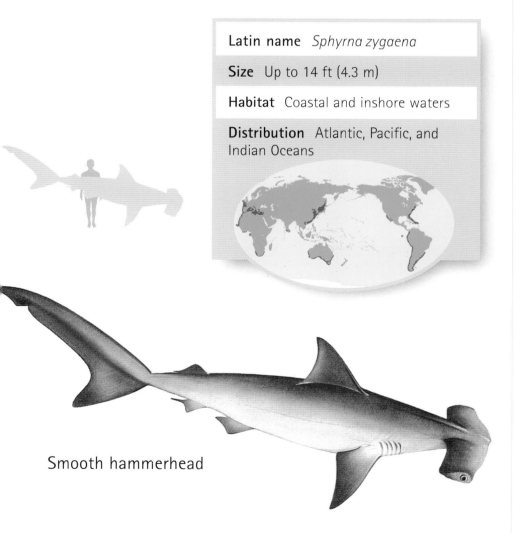

Smooth hammerhead

Basking shark

The basking shark is the second-largest living species of fish. It shares the streamlined body shape of other sharks but its gill slits are extra-large. It feeds entirely on plankton, which it sieves from the water. The shark simply swims with its mouth open, taking in water and plankton. Basking sharks often float sluggishly at the surface of the water.

Greenland shark

The Greenland shark is the giant of its group, which also contains the world's smallest sharks. It appears to be a slow-moving bottom dweller, but will come to the surface in search of food, particularly during the winter. It preys on many kinds of fish and also feeds on mollusks, crustaceans, and squid, and, possibly, on seals and seabirds.

Porbeagle shark

Latin name *Lamina nasus*

Size 6–10ft ft (1.8–3 m)

Habitat Open sea; coastal waters

Distribution N. Atlantic, S. Pacific, Indian Oceans

Greenland shark

Latin name *Somniosus microcephalus*

Size Up to 21 ft (6.4 m)

Habitat Sea bed

Distribution N. Atlantic Ocean: inside Arctic Circle, south to Gulf of Maine and Britain

Porbeagle shark

The porbeagle is a swift-swimming shark that mostly feeds on surface-dwelling fish, such as mackerel and herring. The body temperature of this shark, like that of the mako and the great white, is higher than that of the surrounding water, an adaptation that improves its swimming efficiency. The eggs hatch inside the mother and she gives birth to fully formed live young a short time later.

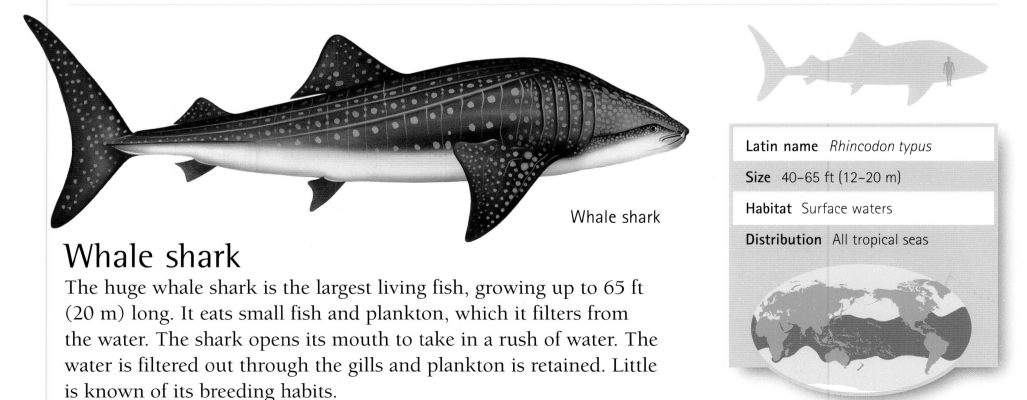

Whale shark

Latin name *Rhincodon typus*

Size 40–65 ft (12–20 m)

Habitat Surface waters

Distribution All tropical seas

Whale shark

The huge whale shark is the largest living fish, growing up to 65 ft (20 m) long. It eats small fish and plankton, which it filters from the water. The shark opens its mouth to take in a rush of water. The water is filtered out through the gills and plankton is retained. Little is known of its breeding habits.

Rays

Like sharks, rays and skates have skeletons made of cartilage. There are about 500 species worldwide. Most live in the oceans in temperate and tropical waters. All, except for the sawfish, have a broad, flattened body and greatly expanded pectoral fins, which extend along the head and trunk, giving the fish a diamond shape. The tail is small and whiplike and the dorsal fins are tiny. The gill openings and slitlike mouth are on the underside of the body.

Atlantic Manta

Southern stingray

Stingrays are almost rectangular and have long, thin tails. The stingray has a sharp venomous spine near the base of the tail, which can inflict a serious wound that may be fatal, even to humans. Stingrays usually live buried in the sand on the sea bed; they feed on fish, crustaceans, and mollusks, which they crush with their strong, flattened teeth.

Latin name	*Manta birostris*
Size	Up to 22 ft (6.8 m) wide
Habitat	Costal waters, open sea
Distribution	Atlantic Ocean: North Carolina to Brazil, Madeira to W. Africa

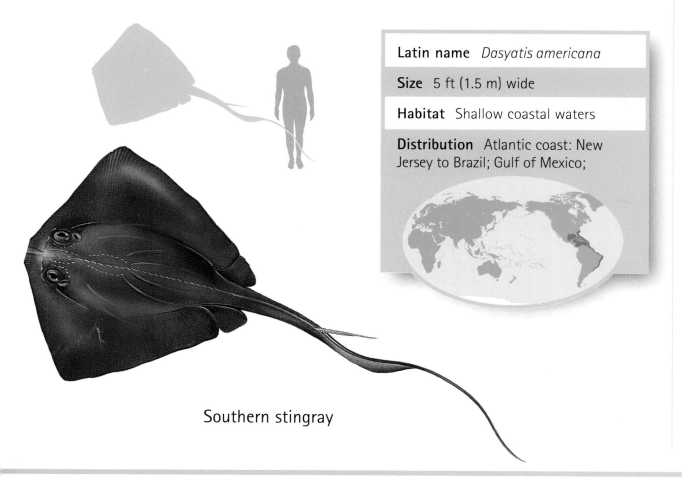

Latin name	*Dasyatis americana*
Size	5 ft (1.5 m) wide
Habitat	Shallow coastal waters
Distribution	Atlantic coast: New Jersey to Brazil; Gulf of Mexico;

Southern stingray

Atlantic manta

The Atlantic manta, also known as the giant devil ray, is the largest ray. Two fleshy projections at each side of its mouth act as scoops for food. Mantas feed on tiny planktonic creatures, which they filter from the water on to their gill arches. They also swallow fish and large crustaceans. The young hatch inside their mother and are born well developed.

Sharks as predators

Sharks are skillful predators, with streamlined bodies, pointed snouts, sharp rows of teeth, and keen senses. When closing in on a kill, a great white shark can race through the water at up to 15 mph (25 km/h), and makos can reach speeds of nearly 20 mph (33 km/h) for short stretches. Many species, such as leopard sharks, have highly flexible bodies that can bend around in small spaces to seek out prey. The thresher shark can even stun prey with a flick of its tail.

Streamlined swimmers

Sharks are agile, graceful swimmers with their beautifully streamlined bodies. They propel themselves through the water by moving their two-vaned tails from side to side. In many sharks, the upper vane of the tail is larger than the lower one, and the front pair of paired fins, the pectorals, act as winglike control surfaces for changing directions. Like the large, unpaired dorsal fins, they also provide directional stability against rolling.

Silvertip shark

Above right: This silvertip shark has large pectoral fins, which enable it to change direction quickly when chasing prey such as eagle rays.

Special senses

Sharks use all their five senses to maximum effect, but they also have a sixth sense. Sensory pores called ampullae of Lorenzini, located in front of the shark's nostrils, allow them to detect weak electrical signals given off by hidden prey. Sharks also use a system of tiny pores that run in a line down each side of their body and onto the head to pick up tiny vibrations made by animals moving through the water. This system of pores, called the lateral line, alerts the shark to the presence of potential prey.

Shark teeth and skin

Sharks' teeth come in many shapes and sizes, depending on the shark's diet. Spiked teeth are used for gripping prey, while serrated teeth are for slicing. Long, curved teeth are used for grasping slippery fish firmly. The teeth continually wear out and are replaced by new ones that grow just behind the front row. Sharks can get through thousands of teeth in a lifetime.

Sharks are covered in small, tooth-like projections called denticles, which give their skin a rough feel. Denticles are shed and replaced by larger ones as the shark grows.

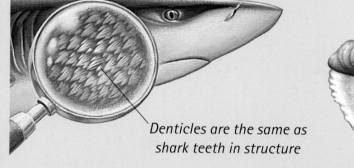

Denticles are the same as shark teeth in structure

CLOSE-UP OF SHARK SKIN

TYPES OF SHARK TEETH

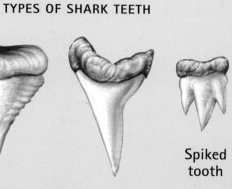

Spiked tooth

Serrated tooth

Curved tooth

Great white shark

Hammerhead shark

Ampullae of Lorenzini detect electrical signals given off by hidden fish

Left: Hammerhead sharks' eyes are located on the end of their head projections. The nostrils are also widely spaced for the greatest possible detection of odors.

Eels

There are more than 730 species of eel, grouped into about 15 families. They occur worldwide, except in polar regions. Most eels are marine, but some live in fresh water. All have long, slender bodies. All species produce eggs that hatch into thin, transparent larvae. Some species live in deep waters. Many species in this order have a large mouth, probably to catch prey larger than themselves. It is thought these eels may attract prey in the darkness of the deep ocean by using a light-producing organ located on the tip of the tail to lure them within striking range.

Conger eel

Latin name	*Conger conger*
Size	Up to 10 ft (3 m)
Habitat	Shallow waters
Distribution	N. Atlantic Ocean: coasts from Iceland to N. Africa; Mediterranean Sea

Conger eel

This large fish is fairly common on rocky shores. It has a large, scaleless, cylindrical body. Its upper jaw overlaps the lower one, giving its face a brutish appearance. The conger eel feeds on fish and crustaceans, particularly crabs, and octopus. Though they are usually found hiding in rock crevices in shallow water, adult congers migrate into deeper water to mate and spawn.

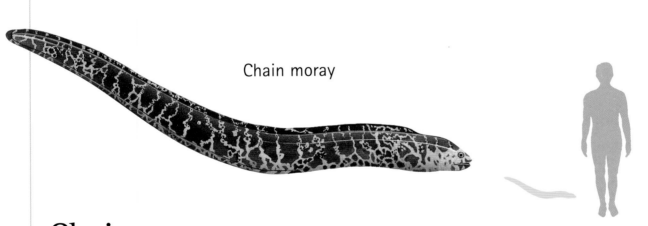

Chain moray

Chain moray

Moray eels of this genus are most abundant in the Indian and Pacific Oceans, but some occur in the tropical Atlantic. The chain moray is common in the Caribbean, where it lives among rocks or rocks and sand, usually in shallow water. Unlike most morays, which have sharp, pointed teeth, the chain moray has blunt teeth. It feeds mainly on crustaceans.

Latin name	*Echidna catenata*
Size	Up to 5 ft (150 cm)
Habitat	Coastal waters
Distribution	W. Atlantic Ocean: Bermuda to Brazil, including Caribbean

Latin name *Muraenidae* family

Size 4¼ ft (1.3 m)

Habitat Rocky shores and coral reefs

Distribution Tropical and subtropical seas

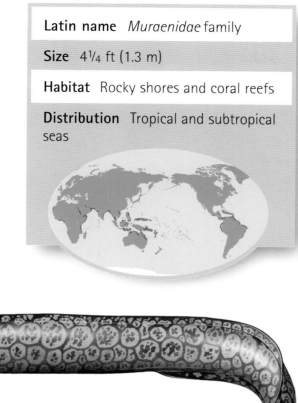

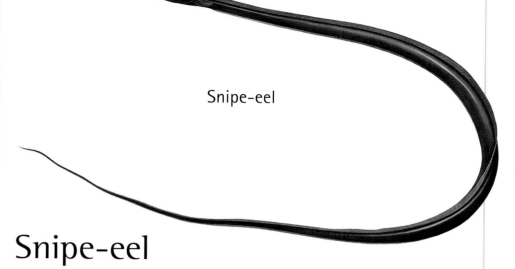

Snipe-eel

Snipe-eel

Snipe-eels are deep-sea fish with immensely long, slender bodies and dorsal and anal fins that run most of the length of their body. The narrow jaws are beaklike and equipped with pointed, backward-facing teeth, which the eel uses to trap prey, such as crustaceans and fish.

Moray

Moray

The 100 species of moray are widely found in tropical and warm temperate oceans. This moray is typical of the group, with its scaleless, boldly patterned body. Its large mouth is equipped with strong, sharp teeth. The moray lurks in underwater rock crevices with only its head showing, watching for prey—largely fish, squid, and cuttlefish.

Latin name *Nemichthys scolopaceus*

Size 3¼–4 ft (1–1.2 m)

Habitat Open ocean

Distribution Atlantic, Pacific, Indian Oceans

Latin name *Anguilla anguilla*

Size 20–40 in (50–100 cm)

Habitat Coastal waters, rivers, streams

Distribution N. Atlantic Ocean, Mediterranean and Black Seas, fresh water in Europe and N. Africa

European eel

The European eel is the only eel-like fish to live in fresh water. Young eels migrate from their freshwater homes to the mid-Atlantic, where they spawn and then die. The European eel is a valuable traditional food-fish and is caught by humans in large quantities. The American eel, found along the Atlantic coasts of North America, closely resembles the European species.

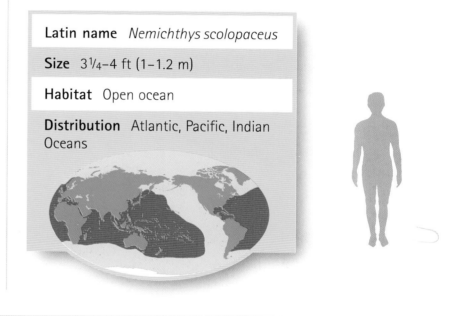

European eel

Herrings

The herring order contains over 350 species of fish. It is one of the most important groups of food-fish—the herring, sardine, and anchovy alone account for a large proportion of the total world fish tonnage. Most fish in this order are marine and live in schools near the surface of the open sea or in inshore waters. Local populations of some species return to traditional spawning grounds. Typically, these fish eat plankton, which they filter from the water through long gill rakers. Their bodies are flattened and covered with large, reflective, silvery scales.

Twaite shad

Latin name	*Alosa fallax*
Size	22 in (55 cm)
Habitat	Open sea, coastal waters
Distribution	Europe, Icelandic coasts, Baltic to Mediterranean Seas

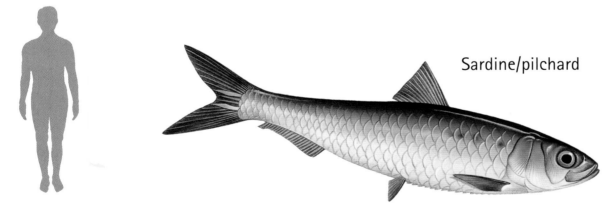

Sardine/pilchard

Sardine/pilchard

The sardine is a herring-like fish but has a more rounded body and larger scales. Its gill covers are marked with distinct radiating ridges. Shoals of sardines move in surface waters and make seasonal migrations northward in summer, south in winter. Young sardines feed mainly on plant plankton, adults on animal plankton. Sardines are extremely valuable food-fish.

Latin name	*Sardina pilchardus*
Size	10 in (25 cm)
Habitat	Open sea, coastal waters
Distribution	European coasts: Mediterranean and Black Seas

Twaite shad

The twaite shad is a heavy-bodied fish with large, fragile scales. Crustaceans and small fish are its main diet. To spawn, the fish migrate from coastal waters to the tidal reaches of rivers, but river pollution and human-made obstructions have affected these journeys badly in some areas. The shads spawn at night, spreading their eggs over the gravel of the river bed.

Wolf herring

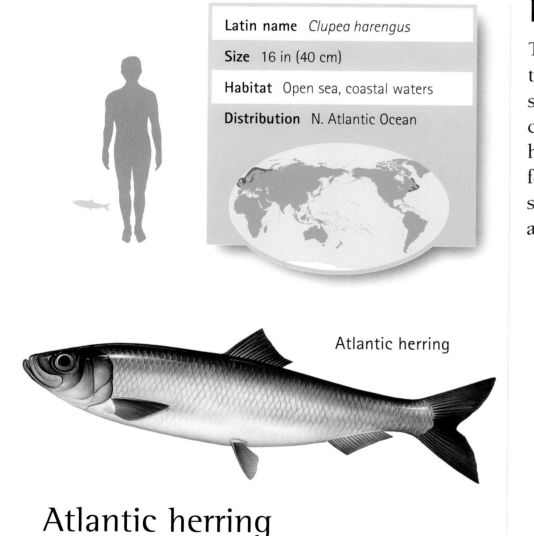

Latin name   *Chirocentrus dorab*

Size   12 ft (3.7 m)

Habitat   Surface waters, shallow sea

Distribution   Indo-Pacific Oceans: Red Sea to Australia

Wolf herring

A herring-like fish of dramatic size—about 5 ft (1.5 m) on average—the wolf herring has a long, cylindrical body and fanglike teeth. It has silvery sides and a bluish back. Unlike other members of the order, it does not filter-feed planktonic food but hunts for fish, crustaceans, squids, and other invertebrates.

Latin name   *Clupea harengus*

Size   16 in (40 cm)

Habitat   Open sea, coastal waters

Distribution   N. Atlantic Ocean

European anchovy

The 110 species of anchovy are found all around the world in temperate to tropical seas. The shape of the anchovy head is distinctive and characteristic, with the snout overhanging the huge mouth. Anchovies are important food items for tuna and many other creatures, and many species are valuable commercial fish. The European anchovy is a slender fish with fragile scales.

European anchovy

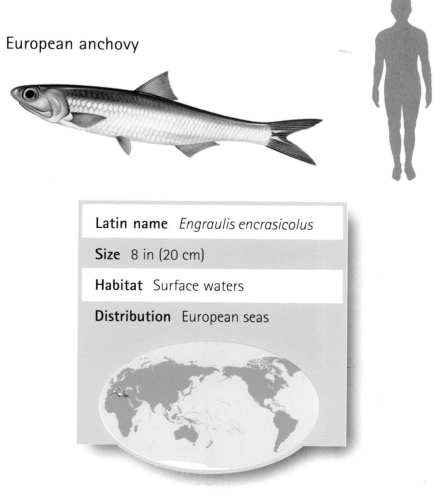

Atlantic herring

Atlantic herring

The Atlantic herring can be divided into a number of races, each with its own characteristics and breeding season. Some races spawn in shallow inshore bays, others offshore on ocean banks. Herrings select different items of planktonic food as they grow and also eat other small crustaceans and small fish. Atlantic herring is an important food-fish and is one of the top commercial species.

Latin name   *Engraulis encrasicolus*

Size   8 in (20 cm)

Habitat   Surface waters

Distribution   European seas

Salmon fish

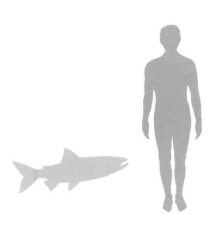

There are about 76 species in the salmonidae family, including salmon, trout, whitefish, graylings, and charrs. Species live in freshwater and marine environments, mainly in the northern hemisphere. Some migrate from the sea into rivers to spawn. At their breeding grounds, the female usually digs a shallow nest in the gravel at the bottom of the river and deposits her eggs, which are then fertilized by the male and covered over. The eggs hatch and the young eventually go out to the sea before returning to the river to spawn. Many species return to the exact same breeding ground with astonishing accuracy.

Lake trout

Lake trout

A popular sport-fishing species in North America, the lake trout is a charr, not a true trout. It has been introduced into lakes out of its natural range. It has pale spots on its head, back, and sides. Lake trout eat fish, insects, crustaceans, and plankton. They spawn in shallow gravel-bottomed water from late summer to December.

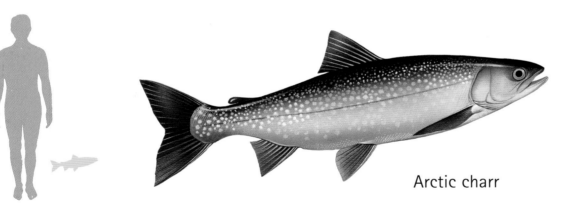

Arctic charr

Arctic charr

The Arctic charr has different habits according to its environment. In the north of its range, it lives in the sea and grows large on a diet of fish, mollusks, and crustaceans. It enters rivers to spawn. Farther south, Arctic charr live in mountain lakes and are much smaller, feeding on crustaceans, insects, larvae, and mollusks.

Latin name	*Salvelinus alpinus*
Size	10–38 in (25–96 cm)
Habitat	Open sea, rivers, lakes
Distribution	Arctic and N. Atlantic Oceans, Europe, Russia, North America

Latin name	*Salvelinus namaycush*
Size	Up to 4 ft (1.2 m)
Habitat	Lakes, rivers
Distribution	Canada, N. U.S.A.

Rainbow trout

Farmed in large quantities, rainbow trout are extremely popular with anglers and are an important food-fish. They feed mainly on insect larvae, mollusks, and crustaceans. Rainbow trout spawn in spring in shallow, gravel-bottomed streams. The female lays her eggs in a shallow nest.

Latin name	*Salmo gairdneri*
Size	Up to 3¼ ft (1 m)
Habitat	Marine; rivers
Distribution	N.W. America, E. Pacific; introduced worldwide

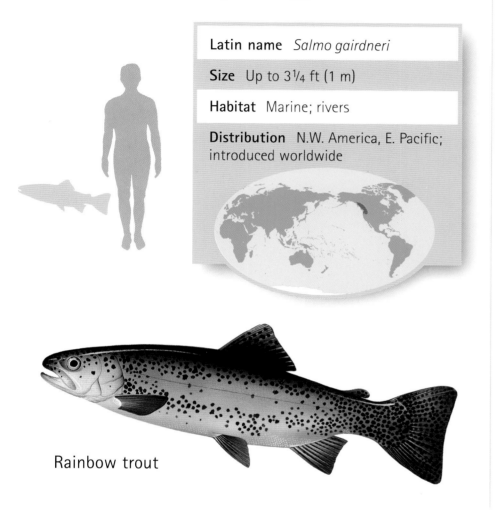

Rainbow trout

Latin name	*Oncorhynchus nerka*
Size	Up to 33 in (84 cm)
Habitat	Seas, rivers, lakes
Distribution	N. Pacific Ocean: North American coast; Alaska to California; coast of Russia to Japan: Hokkaido

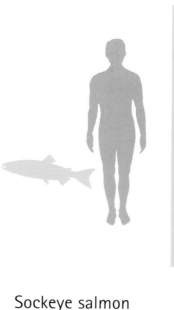

Sockeye salmon

Sockeye salmon

The sockeye salmon lives in the ocean, where it eats small shrimp-like creatures until it is 4 to 6 years old. In late spring, mature adults enter rivers to swim to their breeding areas, sometimes 1,500 miles (2,400 km) inland. The female digs a shallow pit in the stream bed with her tail and body and lays her eggs. After spawning, the adults die.

Atlantic salmon

The Atlantic salmon is a long-bodied, rounded fish with a slightly forked tail. Most migrate from the rivers in which they are born out to sea and then back to the river to spawn. The salmon enter the river at different times but all spawn in the winter. The female lays her eggs in a shallow nest in the river bed.

Latin name	*Salmo salar*
Size	Up to 5 ft (1.5 m)
Habitat	Open sea; rivers
Distribution	N. Atlantic Ocean: Greenland to Cape Cod; Arctic coast of Russia, south to N. Spain

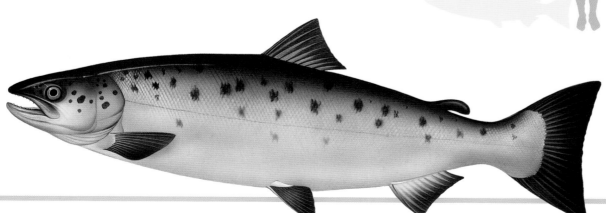

Atlantic salmon

Codfish

The cod order contains about 480 species, only five of which are freshwater fish. They are grouped into 12 families, and some of the most familiar species, such as cod, haddock, whiting, and hake, are extremely valuable food-fish. Most cod species live in the northern hemisphere in relatively shallow waters. Some species in the order, however, notably the grenadiers, live in deep oceanic water. All species feed on fish, crustaceans, and other forms of marine life. Their bodies are covered with small scales. Many members of the order have a sensory barb on the chin. The barb is equipped with additional taste-buds.

Rough-head grenadier

Latin name	*Macrourus berglax*
Size	3–3¼ ft (90–100 cm)
Habitat	Deep water
Distribution	N. Atlantic Ocean: Nova Scotia to Greenland, Iceland, Norway

Atlantic cod

Atlantic cod

The cod has three dorsal fins, two anal fins, and a single, long barbel on its chin. Its large mouth contains many small teeth. Cod usually swim in schools in surface waters but sometimes search for food such as crustaceans, worms, and fish at mid-depths or on the sea bed. The cod is a food-fish that has been caught for centuries.

Latin name	*Gadus morhua*
Size	4 ft (1.2 m)
Habitat	Coastal waters
Distribution	N. Atlantic Ocean: Greenland and Hudson strait to North Carolina; Baltic sea to Bay of Biscay

Rough-head grenadier

The rough-head grenadier is one of a family of about 15 species belonging to the cod order, which are found in deep water; all are known as grenadiers or rat-tails. The males of many of the species can make loud sounds, which they use to communicate. The grenadier feeds on crustaceans, mollusks, and brittlestars.

Latin name *Lota lota*

Size 20–40 in (50–100 cm)

Habitat Rivers, lakes

Distribution Canada, N. U.S.A., N. Europe, Asia

Burbot

The burbot is one of the few fish in the cod order that lives in fresh water. It is a sluggish fish that hides by day and emerges at dawn and dusk to feed. Adults eat fish, crustaceans, and insects, while the young burbot feed on insect larvae and small crustaceans.

Burbot

Whiting

The whiting has three dorsal fins and two anal fins, the first of which is long-based. The upper jaw is longer than the lower. Adult whiting eat fish and crustaceans, while their young feed on small crustaceans. They spawn in spring in shallow water. This common species is a valuable commercial food-fish for humans and is also hunted and eaten by many larger fish and birds.

Latin name *Merlangius merlangus*

Size 12–16 in (30–40 cm)

Habitat Shallow inshore waters

Distribution European coasts, Iceland to Spain, Mediterranean and Black Seas

European hake

Whiting

Latin name *Merluccius merluccius*

Size 3¼–6 ft (1–1.8 m)

Habitat Deep water

Distribution N. Atlantic Ocean: Iceland, Norway to N. Africa; Mediterranean

European hake

True hakes are a small family of codlike fish. The European hake is typical with its slender body, large head, and two dorsal fins, the first of which is triangular and the second long-based and curving. It lives near the sea bed, migrating upward nightly to feed nearer the surface. Hakes spawn in spring and summer. The Pacific hake is similar to the European species in appearance and habits.

Toadfish and anglerfish

Latin name	*Himantolophus groenlandicus*
Size	24 in (60 cm)
Habitat	Deep sea
Distribution	Worldwide (but uncommon)

Toadfish are bottom-dwelling fish found in many of the oceans of the world, mostly in tropical or warm temperate areas. There are about 69 species. The common name comes from the resemblance of the broad, flattened head, with its wide mouth and slightly out-sticking eyes, to that of a toad.

The 300 or so species of anglerfish are found at all depths in tropical and temperate seas. They have large heads, wide mouths filled with many rows of sharp teeth, and small gills. Most anglers have a fishing lure positioned in front of their mouths to attract prey.

Football-fish

Atlantic midshipman

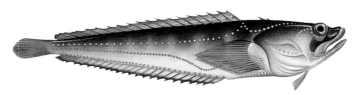

Atlantic midshipman

The bottom-dwelling Atlantic midshipman has a large, flattened head and eyes near the top of the head. The body is scaleless, and on each side there are rows of hundreds of light-producing organs. Also known as the singing fish, this species can make a variety of sounds, including grunts and whistles.

Latin name	*Porichthys porosissimus*
Size	12 in (30 cm)
Habitat	Inshore waters
Distribution	W. Atlantic Ocean: coasts of E. U.S.A. to Argentina

Football-fish

The football-fish is a deep-sea angler. The female is much larger than the male. Its almost spherical body is studded with bony plates, and the modified ray on its head makes a thick "fishing rod," tipped with a many-branched lure and with a central luminous bulb. It preys on fish attracted to the lure.

Sargassumfish

The sargassumfish has a balloon-shaped body covered with bumps and flaps of skin. It is perfectly camouflaged to blend with the sargassum weed in which it lives. Its exact coloration varies, but it always matches its own particular weed patch. It feeds on small invertebrates, which it attracts with the small lure on its snout.

Longlure frogfish

Latin name *Histrio histrio*

Size 8 in (20 cm)

Habitat Surface waters

Distribution Atlantic, Indian, Pacific Oceans, tropical areas

Latin name *Antennarius multiocellatus*

Size 6 in (15 cm)

Habitat Sea bed

Distribution Tropical W. Atlantic Ocean, Caribbean

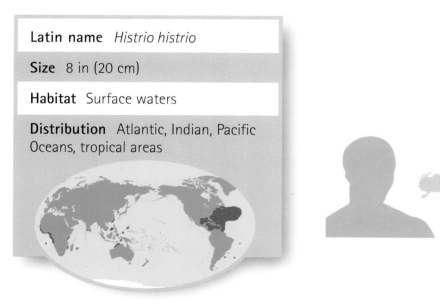

Sargassumfish

Longlure frogfish

The longlure frogfish has a stout body and a pronounced "fishing line" on its snout. Its coloration is variable but it always merges well with its surroundings, whether rock, coral, or seaweed. A bottom-living, slow-moving fish, it crawls around the sea bed with the aid of its limblike pectoral fins, feeding on small fish and crustaceans.

Linophryne arborifera

One of a family of deep-sea anglers, *Linophryne* has a rounded body and a branched chin barbel, which resembles a piece of seaweed. The prominent "fishing rod" on its snout is branched and bears a luminous lure, for attracting prey in the dark deep waters. The tiny adult males are believed to live parasitically on the female, losing their own powers of vision and smell.

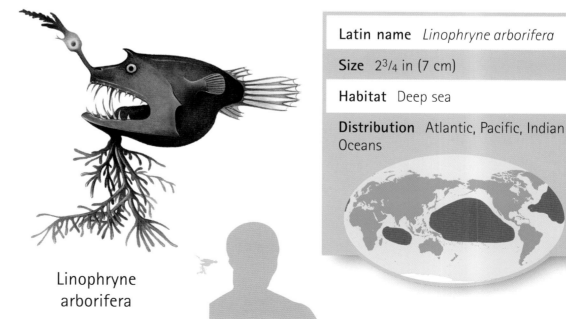

Linophryne arborifera

Latin name *Linophryne arborifera*

Size 2³/₄ in (7 cm)

Habitat Deep sea

Distribution Atlantic, Pacific, Indian Oceans

Fangtooth fish

Life in the deep

Deep-sea fish live in a zone of the ocean that receives no sunlight from above. Light travels only a few hundred meters below the water surface, so about 90 percent of the ocean volume is invisible to humans. The deep sea is also an extremely hostile environment, with massive pressures and low temperatures. Deep-sea fish have adapted to these conditions, and are some of the strangest looking creatures on Earth.

Mysterious fish

The fish that live in the harsh environments of the deep ocean cannot survive in the environments with which humans are familiar, and any attempts to keep them in captivity have led to their deaths. Studying them using deep-sea exploratory equipment is highly expensive. For these reasons, little is known about them, and many species are known only to scientists.

Adaptations

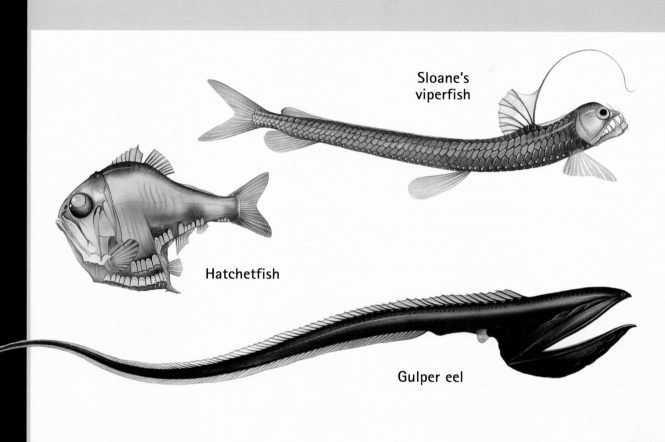

Sloane's viperfish

Hatchetfish

Gulper eel

With no natural light in the deep ocean, fish cannot rely on their eyesight for locating prey and mates and avoiding predators. Many species, like Sloane's viperfish and the hatchetfish, are bioluminescent (light-producing), with large eyes adapted to the dark, and long feelers to help them locate prey or attract mates. Species like the gulper eel have huge jaws to engulf any fish or crustaceans that swim in.

Left: Fangtooth fish normally live at depths of up to 16,000 ft (5,000 m) by day, but search for food nearer to the surface each night.

Bottom feeders

With very little able to survive in the deep-sea environment, most fish that live there rely on dead fish or algae sinking down from above. With less to survive on, deep-sea fish are smaller and have larger mouths and guts than surface fish. The fish that live at the deepest levels have jellylike flesh and basic bone structure. This makes them slower and less agile than surface fish.

Perchlike fish

This is the largest and most varied of all fish orders and contains more species than any other vertebrate order. There are 148 families and at least 9,300 species known. Perchlike fish live in almost every type of aquatic habitat and in doing so have evolved a diverse range of body forms and habits. They include species as different as the dolphinfish, the clownfish, and the swordfish. Perhaps as many as three-quarters of the species live in waters close to the shore. There are 18 suborders of perchlike fish.

Latin name	*Lates niloticus*
Size	6½ ft (2 m)
Habitat	Rivers, lakes
Distribution	Africa: Congo, Volta, and Niger river systems, Lake Chad

Dolphinfish

Nile perch

The Nile perch is widely found in Africa and has been introduced into many artificial lakes. It is fished commercially and for sport and is one of the most important food-fish in some regions of Africa. A large, heavy-bodied fish, the Nile perch has the spiny first dorsal fin characteristic of the perchlike fish and three spines on the anal fin. It eats mainly fish.

Dolphinfish

The dolphinfish is immediately identifiable, with its long dorsal fin that begins above its head and covers the length of its spine. It is colored in vivid blue, green, and yellow hues. These fish move in small schools and feed on other fish, squid, and crustaceans. They are popular game fish and excellent to eat.

Latin name	*Coryphaena hippurus*
Size	Up to 5 ft (1.5 m)
Habitat	Open sea
Distribution	Atlantic, Pacific, Indian Oceans

Clown anemonefish

Unmistakable with its broad bands of white and orange and its dark-rimmed fins, the clown anemonefish has developed a relationship with large sea anemones, living among their stinging tentacles. The fish shelters here from predators and is protected from the anemone's poison by its own body mucus. It feeds on tiny crustaceans and other organisms.

Latin name	*Amphiprion percula*
Size	2¼ in (6 cm)
Habitat	Coral reefs
Distribution	W. and Central Pacific Ocean

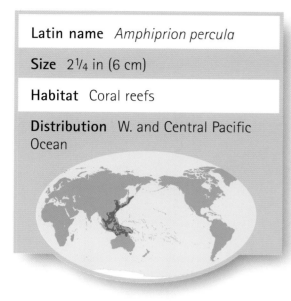

Clown anemonefish

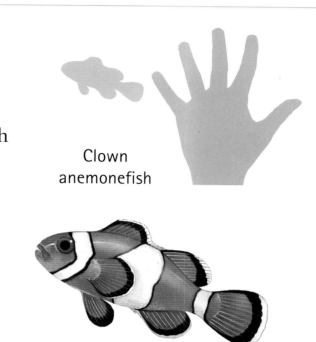

Atlantic blue marlin

The blue marlin weighs at least 400 lb (180 kg) on average and can be more than twice as heavy. It uses its long snout to stun prey such as schooling fish and squid. Blue marlins are among the fastest of all fish and have streamlined bodies. They make regular seasonal migrations, moving toward the equator in winter and away again in summer.

Latin name	*Makaira nigricans*
Size	10–15 ft (3-4.6 m)
Habitat	Offshore waters, open sea
Distribution	Atlantic Ocean, tropical and warm temperate areas

Latin name	*Xiphias gladius*
Size	6½–16 ft (2-5 m)
Habitat	Open sea
Distribution	Worldwide, temperate and tropical seas

Swordfish

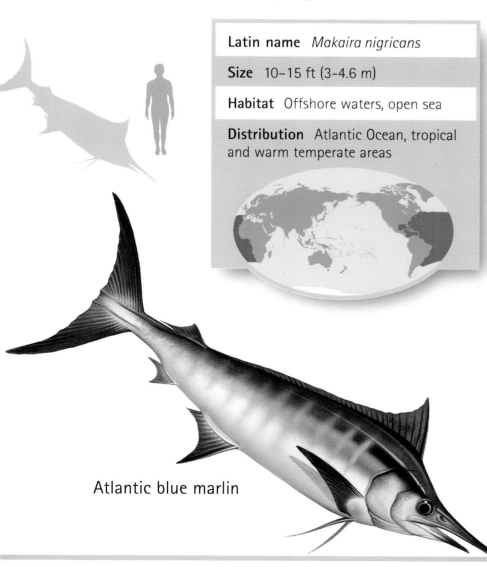

Atlantic blue marlin

Swordfish

The huge and spectacular swordfish is generally solitary and does not form schools, except in the spawning season. It is a fast, active predator and feeds on a variety of small fish and squids. The exact function of the sword is not clear; it may be used to strike at schooling fish, or it may be simply a result of body streamlining.

Flatfish

This group contains 11 families and about 750 species, all but three of which are marine. The typical flatfish has a compressed body and spends much of its life on the sea bed. Most species spawn at a particular time of year, laying eggs in the water, where they hatch and the larvae develop. Young flatfish swim normally, but as they develop, the eye on one side moves to the other side and the fish then swims on its side with both eyes facing upward. It also lies on the seabed in this position. Bone structure, nerves, and muscles undergo complex modifications to achieve this change. All flatfish are bottom-feeding predators.

Turbot

Turbot

The turbot is an extremely broad flatfish, with a large head and mouth; the female is bigger than the male. Its scaleless body is usually brownish, with dark speckles that camouflage it on the sea bed. Most turbots have both eyes on the left side. Adults are active predators, feeding largely on young fish. Turbot is one of the finest and most commercially valuable food-fish.

Summer flounder

Summer flounder

The summer flounder is a slender, active flatfish, with both eyes normally on the left side of its head. It feeds on crustaceans, mollusks, and fish. It is a relatively fast swimmer, but much of its life is spent lying half-buried on the sea bed. Its coloration varies according to the type of bottom it is lying on.

Latin name *Paralichthys dentatus*

Size Up to 3¼ ft (1 m)

Habitat Coastal waters, bays, harbors

Distribution W. Atlantic Ocean: Maine to South Carolina

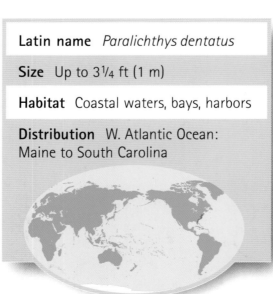

Latin name *Scophthalmus maximus*

Size 3¼ ft (1 m)

Habitat Shallow inshore waters

Distribution E. Atlantic Ocean: Sardinia, Britain, south to N. Africa; Mediterranean

American plaice

Also known as the long rough dab, this plaice has toothed scales on its eyed side, which gives the skin a rough texture. Both of the eyes are on the right side, which is brown or reddish-brown. The underside is white. American plaice live on sand or mud bottoms, feeding on invertebrates.

American plaice

Latin name	*Paralichthys californicus*

Size 5 ft (1.5 m)

Habitat Sandy-bottomed coastal waters

Distribution Pacific Ocean: coast of California, sometimes as far north as Oregon

California halibut

Latin name	*Hippoglossoides platessoides*

Size 12–24 in (30–60 cm)

Habitat Depths of 130–600 ft (40–180 m)

Distribution W. Atlantic Ocean: Greenland, Labrador, south to Rhode Island; E. Atlantic: Iceland, Barents Sea, English Channel

California halibut

The California halibut is a member of the lefteye flounder family, but perhaps as much as half the population have both eyes on the right side. It feeds on fish, particularly anchovies, and has a large mouth and strong teeth. The halibut, in turn, is eaten by rays, sea lions, and porpoises and is also an important commercial food-fish for humans. Spawning occurs in spring and early summer.

Blackcheek tonguefish

The blackcheek tonguefish has a body that is broadest at the front and tapers to a pointed tail. Its dorsal and anal fins unite with the tail, but it has no pectoral fins, and only the left pelvic fin is developed. Both of the eyes are on the left of the head, and the small mouth is contorted to the left.

Latin name	*Symphurus plagusia*

Size 8 in (20 cm)

Habitat Sandy bays, estuaries

Distribution W. Atlantic Ocean: New York, south to Florida, Bahamas, and Gulf of Mexico

Blackcheek tonguefish

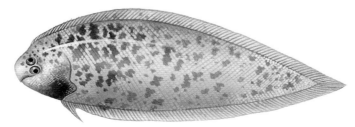

Coelacanths and lungfish

Coelacanths are sarcopterygian (lobe-finned) fish that, together with lungfish, are the closest living relatives of four-limbed land vertebrates (tetrapods). Their lobed fins, like tetrapod limbs, are supported by an internal skeleton. The few living members of the class include the coelacanth and the lungfish. There is a single living species of coelacanth, yet this order was once widespread and abundant. Coelacanths were only known as 90-million-year-old fossils until one was caught by a fisherman off the coast of South Africa in 1938. Lungfish have lunglike breathing organs, which they can use to take breaths of air at the surface. Underwater, they inhale water as other fish do.

Latin name	*Latimeria chalumnae*
Size	6¼ ft (1.9 m)
Habitat	Rocky or coral slopes
Distribution	Indian Ocean, off Comoros Islands; off Sulawesi

Coelacanth

Coelacanths are heavy-bodied fish, with fleshy lobes at the base of all fins except the first dorsal fin; the pectoral fins can be turned through 180 degrees. The heart is extremely simple compared to the heart of other fish and the kidneys are positioned on the underside of the body, unlike those of any other vertebrate. Modern coelacanths are carnivores that feed mainly on fish. They bear fully formed young that hatch from eggs inside the mother.

Coelacanth

South American lungfish

The South American lungfish has a pair of lunglike organs connected to its windpipe. This fish usually lives in oxygen-poor, swampy areas, so it uses its lungs to supplement the oxygen obtained from the water by breathing air at the surface. During dry seasons, when the swamp dries out, the lungfish survives by digging itself a burrow in which it lives, breathing air. It closes the burrow entrance with mud and covers itself with a mucus secretion to conserve moisture. The body slows down to a dormant state.

Latin name	*Lepidosiren paradoxa*
Size	4 ft (1.2 m)
Habitat	Swamps, weeded river margins
Distribution	C. South America

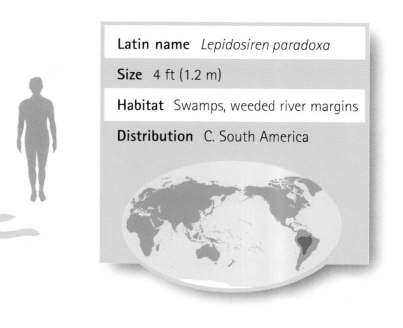

Latin name	*Protopterus aethiopicus*
Size	6½ ft (2 m) long
Habitat	Rivers, lakes
Distribution	E. and C. Africa

African lungfish

Australian lungfish

First discovered in 1870, the Australian lungfish differs from other lungfish in that it has only one lung. The waters it lives in do not dry up and so it does not need to hibernate, unlike some other lungfish. In captivity it is mainly carnivorous and feeds on almost any animal food. The fish spawns from August to October in shallow water.

Latin name	*Neoceratodus forsteri*
Size	5ft (1.5 m)
Habitat	Rivers
Distribution	Australia: Queensland

African lungfish

The African lungfish has a pair of lungs connected to its windpipe and can breathe air at the water surface. Its gills are poorly developed. The lungfish comes to the surface to breathe about every 30 minutes. In dry periods it can burrow and hibernate like the South American lungfish. The female lays eggs in a hole that the male has made.

Australian lungfish

Insects and arachnids

Insects outnumber every other animal on Earth. There are about 1.5 million known animal species in the world, and about one million of those species are insects. Insects have colonized every type of habitat, except the ocean, and eat every imaginable type of food.

Specialized structures

One reason for the success of insects is that their basic body structure has adapted well to a huge variety of environments and lifestyles. For example, every insect has mouthparts made up of several paired structures, which have evolved to help different insects eat in a specific way, including chewing, piercing and sucking, and siphoning. Insect legs are also specialized for activities such as jumping, swimming, digging, or running. Arachnids, which include spiders and scorpions, are not insects but an entirely separate group.

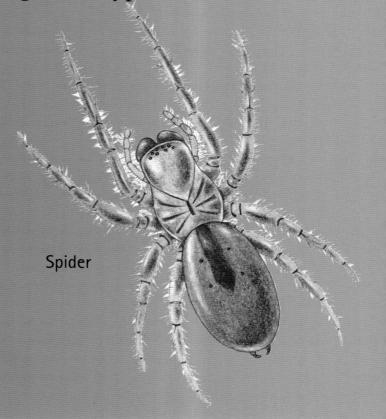
Spider

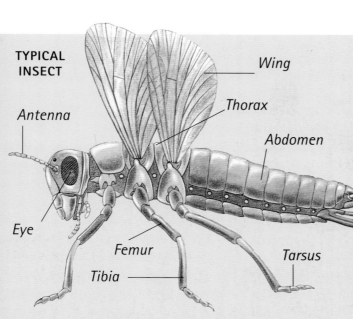

TYPICAL INSECT

Antenna

Wing

Thorax

Abdomen

Eye

Femur

Tibia

Tarsus

Insect body parts

Although insects are incredibly varied they can be identified by certain features. An insect's body is divided into three parts—head, thorax, and abdomen. The head carries the eyes, mouthparts, and a pair of sensory antennae, which the insect uses to find out about its surroundings. On the thorax are the insect's three pairs of legs and, usually, two pairs of wings. The abdomen contains the reproductive organs and most of the digestive system. The insect's body is protected by a supporting structure called the exoskeleton.

Cockroaches, earwigs, and grasshoppers

Among the most adaptable of all creatures, these insects live everywhere from the tops of mountains to city houses. While these insects are not closely related, they share certain features. All of them are strong-jawed, chewing creatures with mobile heads and most have large hind wings. They also share a long ancestry—cockroaches date back some 350 million years. Many of these insects share an ability to conceal themselves from enemies by blending into their surroundings. Most are considered pests by humans.

Madagascan hissing cockroach

Latin name	Gromphadorhina portentosa
Size	2–3 in (5–7.5 cm)
Habitat	Tropical dry forest, rainforest
Distribution	Madagascar

American cockroach

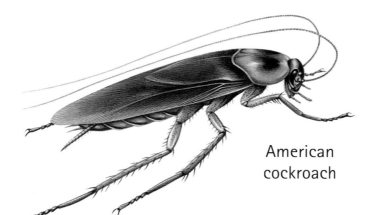

American cockroach

Commonly living in buildings, the American cockroach hides by day and feeds on decaying organic matter or anything else it can find by night. The female deposits her eggs into a purse-shaped container, which is attached to her body. She leaves this egg case in a dark, safe place before the eggs hatch.

Latin name	Periplaneta americana
Size	3/4–2 in (2–5 cm)
Habitat	Varied
Distribution	North America

Madagascan hissing cockroach

This large, wingless cockroach makes a hissing sound through breathing holes in its abdomen when alarmed. It has a brown segmented abdomen and a darker brown thorax. Females have two short antennae that point downward. Males have two longer antennae that point upward.

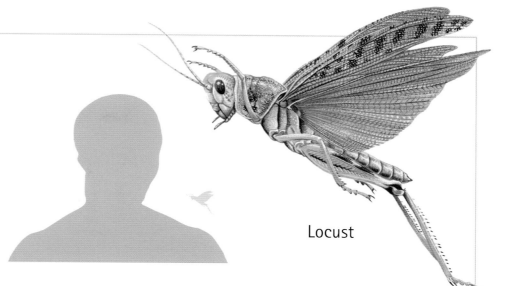

Locust

Locust

Locust is the name given to the swarming phase of short-horned grasshoppers of the family *Acrididae*. Huge swarms of adult locusts can travel great distances and swoop down onto crops, feeding until there are scarcely any leaves left. A single swarm may contain billions of insects.

Striped earwig

Also known as the long-horned earwig, the striped earwig stays hidden during the day and comes out at night to hunt other insects. If attacked it can squirt out a bad-smelling liquid from special glands on the abdomen. It has large wings that have to be folded many times in order to fit under the small front wings.

Striped earwig

Short-horned grasshopper

Short-horned grasshopper

Short-horned grasshoppers, which include locusts, have short antennae, large heads, and big eyes. Most have two pairs of wings, though they are not strong fliers, spending most of their lives on the ground. They make a loud song by rubbing their wings together and can leap into the air if frightened.

Mantids and dragonflies

Flower mantis

Mantids, dragonflies, and their relatives are some of the fiercest insect predators. Mantids are well known for their expert hunting techniques. They are equipped with long front legs, which they extend at lightning speed to grasp their prey. More energetic hunters are the dragonflies, some of the fastest-flying of all insects. They seize their prey in the air or pluck tiny creatures from leaves. They spend much of their lives as aquatic nymphs, which hunt for worms, tadpoles, insects, and even tiny fish.

Latin name	*Creobroter*
Size	1¼–2 in (3–5 cm)
Habitat	Vegetation
Distribution	W. Asia

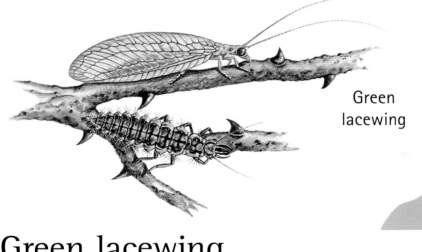

Green lacewing

Green lacewing

This species is one of a number of lacewings found in gardens. It has a bluish-green body, large golden or copper-bronze eyes, and turns a purplish or brownish pink in the fall, when it often enters houses to spend the winter in a cool room. Green lacewings eat aphids on the foliage of shrubs and trees—which benefits gardeners.

Latin name	*Chrysoperla carnea*
Size	⅜–¾ in (1–2 cm)
Habitat	Vegetation
Distribution	N.E., Mid-W., and W. U.S.A., Europe

Flower mantis

Different species of flower mantis are differently colored to match the flowers they perch on. This helps them stay hidden from both their victims and their enemies. Some species resemble ants during their early nymph stages, as a defense against predators such as birds and wasps—since most ants are aggressive and unpleasant to eat.

Damselfly

Damselflies appear similar to dragonflies, but when at rest the adult damselfly holds its wings partly spread, unlike the dragonfly, and it is also known as the spread-winged damselfly. Damselflies live around ponds and marshes, where they catch insects such as aphids.

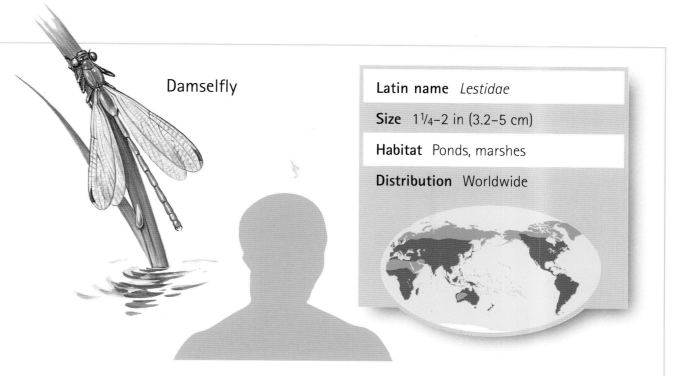

Damselfly

Latin name	*Lestidae*
Size	1¼–2 in (3.2–5 cm)
Habitat	Ponds, marshes
Distribution	Worldwide

Latin name	*Libellulidae*
Size	1–3 in (2.5–7.7 cm)
Habitat	Still or slow-moving water
Distribution	Worldwide

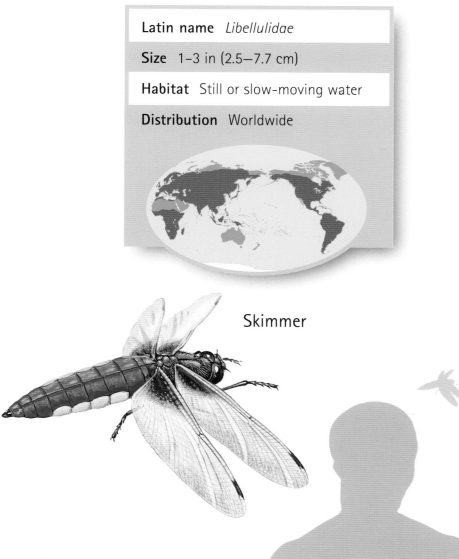

Skimmer

Emperor dragonfly

The emperor dragonfly is a large, powerful species of European hawker dragonfly. It hunts for small insects over water, swooping and darting with amazing speed and agility. Males have a turquoise-blue abdomen marked with a black dorsal stripe and an apple-green thorax. Females have a dullish green thorax and abdomen.

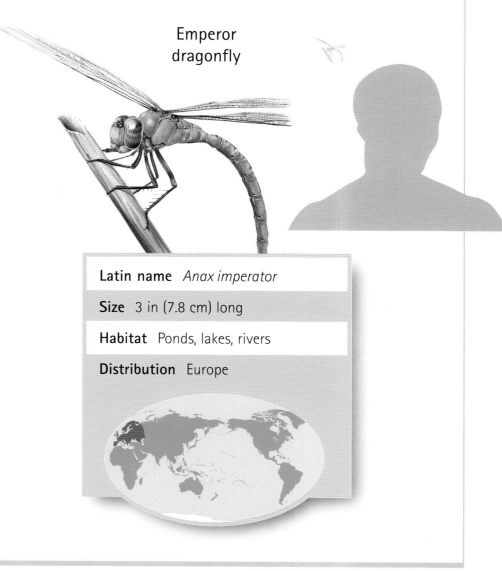

Emperor dragonfly

Latin name	*Anax imperator*
Size	3 in (7.8 cm) long
Habitat	Ponds, lakes, rivers
Distribution	Europe

Skimmer

Skimmers are the most common and colorful members of the dragonfly family. Their wide, flattened bodies are shorter than their wings. Some skimmers have a wingspan of up to 4 in (10 cm). Skimmers are usually seen near still or slow-moving water, where they feed on mosquitoes, flies, and other flying insects.

Bugs, lice, and fleas

Cicada

Although the name bug is used for insects generally, it can also describe a particular group of insects. These include a wide variety of species such as stinkbugs, cicadas, and aphids. All of these insects have special mouthparts for piercing food sources and sucking out the juices. Lice and fleas are two other groups of insects that live as parasites. Small, wingless lice live on birds and mammals. They feed on skin, hair, feathers, or blood. Fleas, too, pierce the skin of birds and mammals and feed on their blood.

Treehopper

Cicada

This insect is best known for the shrill, almost constant call made by the males. The sound is produced by a pair of structures called tymbals, located on the abdomen, which are vibrated by special muscles. Female cicadas usually lay their eggs in slits they make in tree branches. The nymphs molt several times before reaching adult size.

Treehopper

There are about 3,000 species of treehoppers. These insects have a strange-shaped extension on their thorax, which makes them look like a thorn on a plant. They feed on sap from trees and other plants. Excess sap attracts ants, which provide some species of treehooper with protection from predators.

Latin name	*Membracidae*
Size	1/4–1/2 in (0.5–1.3 cm)
Habitat	Rainforest, temperate forest
Distribution	Worldwide

Latin name	*Cicadidae*
Size	1–2 in (2–5 cm)
Habitat	Temperate and tropical areas
Distribution	Worldwide

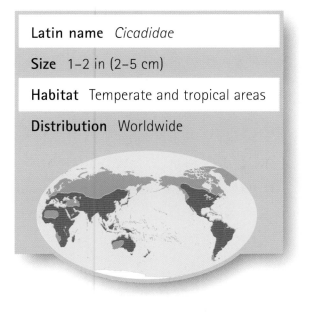

Stinkbug

Shield-shaped in adult form, stinkbugs get their name from the foul-smelling liquid they squirt at any creature that threatens them. The liquid comes from glands on the underside of the stinkbug's body. They feed on the developing seeds of many plants, and when grouped in large numbers can cause extensive damage to cultivated crops.

Latin name	Acrosternum hilare
Size	½–¾ in (1.4—2 cm)
Habitat	Woodland, cultivated land
Distribution	North America

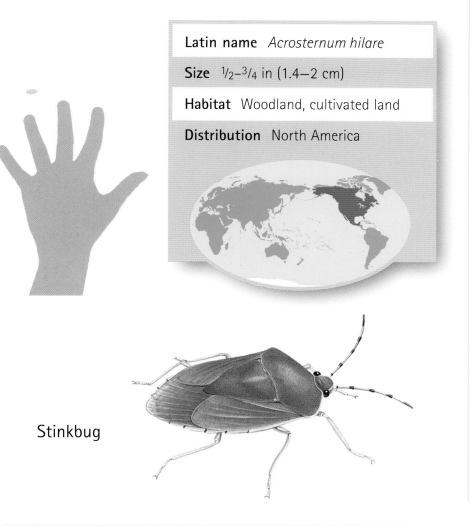

Stinkbug

Latin name	Ctenocephalides felis
Size	Up to ¼ in (7 mm) long
Habitat	Cats, dogs
Distribution	Worldwide

Cat flea

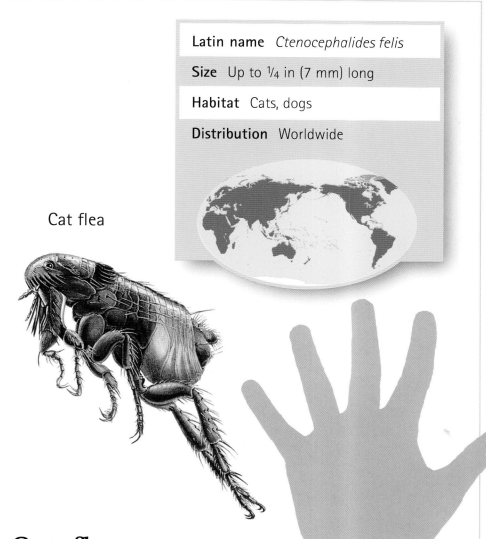

Cat flea

The cat flea is one of the most widespread fleas in the world. Like most fleas, the cat flea can jump up to 200 times its length. This helps it leap onto cats (and sometimes dogs) to feed on their blood. The spiny combs on the flea's head help to anchor it in the cat's fur. The female lays her eggs on the cat, where they hatch into larvae.

Head louse

The head louse is a sucking louse that lives on human heads, feeding on blood. It holds onto hairs with its large, strong front legs and claws and also glues its eggs to the hairs of its host. A female can lay between 50 and 150 eggs in its life, but it can lay up to 100 eggs in 30 days. The adult head louse appears flat when viewed from the side and is tan to grayish-white in color.

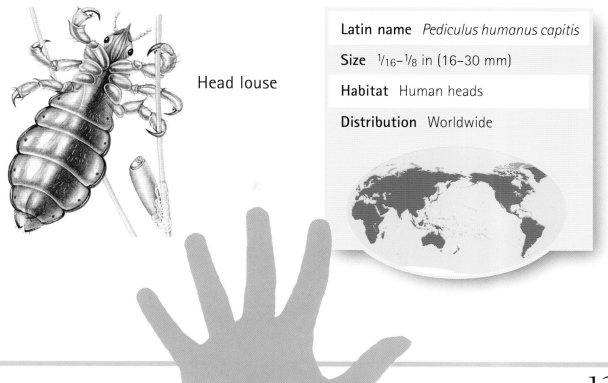

Head louse

Latin name	Pediculus humanus capitis
Size	1/16–⅛ in (16–30 mm)
Habitat	Human heads
Distribution	Worldwide

137

Butterflies and moths

Atlas moth

Butterflies and moths form the second largest insect group, with about 150,000 species. Butterflies and moths are similar in structure. All have two pairs of wings covered in tiny, often colorful scales. They have large eyes, and most have a long, tubular mouthpart called a proboscis to suck up nectar, tree sap, and other liquids. Generally, butterflies are brightly patterned, day-flying creatures while moths are much duller and fly at night, though there are many exceptions. The larvae, called caterpillars, feed on plants, before becoming pupae and emerging as the winged adult.

Latin name	*Attacus atlas*
Size	Wingspan: 10–12 in (25-30 cm)
Habitat	Tropical and subtropical forests
Distribution	Southeast Asia, southern China, Malay archipelago to Indonesia

Luna moth

Luna moth

With a wingspan of 4½–5 in (11.5–12.5 cm), luna moths are one of the largest and most unusual moths. They are green-yellow in color, with long tails. An adult moth lives for only about one week. It has no mouth and does not eat, existing only to mate and produce two generations a year.

Latin name	*Actias luna*
Size	Wingspan: 4½–5 in (11.5–13 cm)
Habitat	Vegetation
Distribution	North America

Atlas moth

The brightly patterned Atlas moth is one of the largest in the world. Most have transparent, scaleless patches on their broad wings. The black eyes on the wing tips may be used to deter predators. Their bodies are hairy and small in proportion to their wings. Males are smaller than females, with more tapered wings, and larger, bushier antennae.

Monarch butterfly

This butterfly has orange-and-black-patterned wings. Females have darker veins on their wings, and males have a spot in the center of each hindwing. Every fall, millions of monarchs fly south from Canada to Mexico—a distance of about 2,000 miles (3,220 km). The following spring, the butterflies lay their eggs as they return north. The caterpillars feed on leaves and buds.

Monarch butterfly

Latin name *Danaus plexippus*

Size Wingspan: 2¼–4 in (5.7–10 cm)

Habitat Vegetation

Distribution North America, New Zealand, Australia, Canary Islands, Madeira, Azores, Portugal, Spain

Fluminense swallowtail butterfly

Swallowtail butterflies differ from all other butterflies in a number of ways. Their caterpillars possess a unique organ behind their heads, which emits smelly secretions when the caterpillar is threatened. The adults are often tailed, giving the insect its name. This species is now endangered.

Fluminense swallowtail butterfly

Latin name *Parides ascanius*

Size Wingspan: 3¼–4¼ in (8–11 cm)

Habitat Coastal swamps

Distribution Rio de Janeiro

Latin name *Ornithoptera alexandrae*

Size Wingspan: up to 12 in (30 cm)

Habitat Rainforest

Distribution Papua New Guinea

Queen Alexandra's birdwing butterfly

Queen Alexandra's birdwing butterfly

The rare Queen Alexandra's birdwing is the largest butterfly in the world, with a wingspan of up to 12 in (30 cm) and a body length of 3 in (8 cm). The butterfly arms itself with a poison, which it gets from a special plant. Adults sip liquid food or nectar from plants using a long, flexible, tubelike "tongue" called a proboscis.

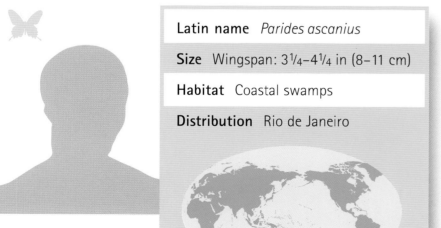

Insect metamorphosis

Metamorphosis is the process by which an insect develops after birth into an adult. There are various stages of metamorphosis, at each of which the insect changes shape and form. Each stage of metamorphosis is usually accompanied by a change of habitat and behavior. Insect growth and metamorphosis are controlled by hormones made by endocrine glands near the front of the body.

Growth stages

In insects, metamorphosis takes place in separate stages, starting with the immature form, called the larva or nymph. A larva either grows in stages, called molts, or becomes inactive and is known as a pupa, or chrysalis, before ending as an adult. In insects that molt, the larvae resemble the adult form but are smaller and, if the adult has wings, wingless. Larvae that pass through the pupa stage look completely different from the adult form. In the pupa stage, the insect builds a protective cocoon around itself. Inside the pupa, the insect transforms into an adult.

Feeding mouthparts

Moth egg to pupa

SPHINX MOTH METAMORPHOSIS

Egg

Egg stage

The larvae of butterflies and moths are called caterpillars. As soon as a caterpillar hatches from its egg it starts to feed, devouring plants with its strong, chewing mouthparts. The caterpillar grows fast and sheds its skin several times as it gets bigger. When fully grown, the caterpillar becomes a pupa. The sphinx moth pupates on the ground in a cocoon made of silk.

Caterpillar stage

Cocoon

Pupa rests in burrow on ground

Pupa stage

Length of metamorphosis

The amount of time spent in each stage of metamorphosis differs from species to species. Some species spend most of their lives as immature forms, living as an adult for relatively short periods. The mayfly, for example, lives for just one day as an adult, existing only to reproduce itself for the next generation. A typical butterfly, however, such as the monarch butterfly, spends about 4 days as an egg, 2 weeks as a caterpillar, 10 days as a pupa, and then lives for 2 to 6 weeks as an adult.

Above: The sphynx moth emerges from its silk cocoon as a fully formed adult. This species of sphynx moth has eye spots on its wings to scare off potential predators.

Sphynx moth

Flies

One of the largest groups of insects, with more than 90,000 known species, flies are common almost everywhere. One of the few land-based creatures to survive in the Antarctic is a midge, a type of fly. An important feature of flies is that they have only one pair of wings or none. On some, the hind wings are reduced to small, knobbed structures called halteres, which help the fly to balance as it flies. Flies usually take liquid food. Most fly larvae are soft, legless creatures, often called maggots, that live in such places as soil, plants, and the bodies of other creatures. The larvae of flies such as mosquitoes live in water and are not maggotlike.

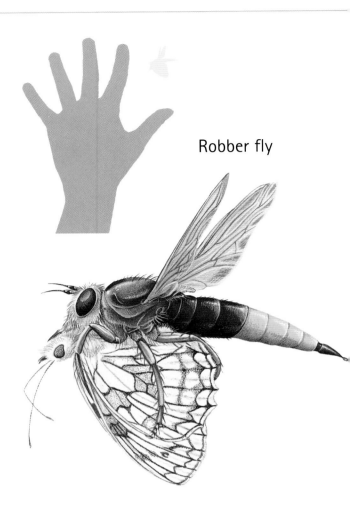
Robber fly

Latin name	*Asilidae* (family)
Size	1/4–1 3/4 in (6–45 mm)
Habitat	Dry, sandy areas
Distribution	Worldwide

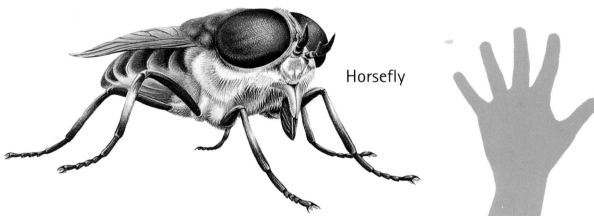
Horsefly

Horsefly

Horseflies are among the world's largest flies and have particularly large, iridescent eyes. Males feed on pollen and nectar but female horseflies take blood from animals, including humans. Their bites can be painful and the flies can carry diseases such as anthrax. There are about 3,000 species, 350 of which are found in North America.

Latin name	*Tabanidae* (family)
Size	1/4–1 in (6–25 mm)
Habitat	Active in hot weather
Distribution	Worldwide

Robber fly

A fast-moving hunter, the robber fly chases and catches other insects in the air or pounces on them on the ground. It has strong, bristly legs for seizing its prey. Once it has caught its victim, the robber fly sucks out its body fluids with its short, sharp mouthparts. Larvae live in soil or rotting wood and feed on the larvae of other insects.

Crane fly

With their long, thin legs, crane flies look like large mosquitoes. Most adults live only a few days and probably do not eat. The larvae feed mainly on plant roots and rotting plants, though some are predators. Unlike mosquitoes, crane flies are weak and poor fliers with a tendency to "wobble" in unpredictable patterns during flight.

Latin name	*Tipulidae* (family)
Size	1/4–2 1/2 in (6–25 mm)
Habitat	Vegetation
Distribution	Worldwide

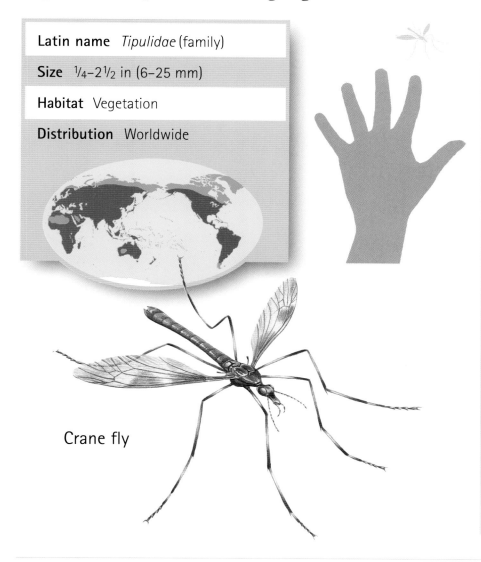

Crane fly

Fruit fly

Latin name	*Drosophila melanogaster*
Size	1/8–3/8 in (3–10 mm) long
Habitat	Vegetation
Distribution	Worldwide

Fruit fly

These little flies are common around flowers and overripe fruit. Their larvae feed on plant matter and some are serious pests, causing great damage to fruit trees and other crops. Fruit flies have red eyes, are yellow-brown in colour, and have black rings along their abdomen. Scientists often use fruit flies for research into biology and genetics.

Mosquito

Mosquitoes' wings beat so fast—about 500 beats a second—that the insects make a constant whining sound as they fly. Males, and sometimes females, feed on nectar and plant sap. Most females also bite and suck the blood of vertebrate animals.

Mosquito

Latin name	*Panthera tigris*
Size	Up to 1/2 in (1.5 cm)
Habitat	Stagnant water, vegetation
Distribution	Worldwide

Beetles

Beetles form the largest of all groups of insects. More than a quarter of a million species are known. Beetles live in almost every type of habitat from polar lands to rainforests. They have strong, chewing mouthparts and feed on almost every type of food. Some hunt ants and other insects. Many eat seeds and wood. Others feed on dung and the fur and flesh of dead animals. Despite their different habits, most beetles have a similar body structure. Their wings are the most characteristic feature. Typically, they have two pairs of wings—the front pair are thick and hard and act as covers for the back wings. When the beetle is at rest, its back pair are folded away under the front wings.

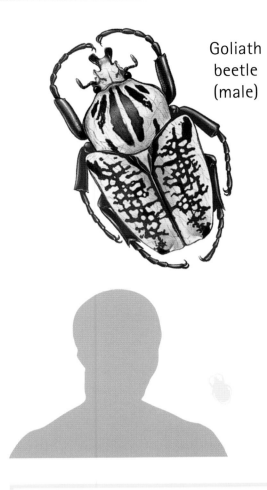

Goliath beetle (male)

Diving beetle

Diving beetle

Diving beetles live in freshwater ponds and streams. They swim by moving their long, paddlelike back legs together like oars. Both adults and larvae hunt prey— even the larvae can capture tadpoles and small fish. This aquatic beetle can also fly, and in spring and autumn it will fly at night in search of new ponds. The female usually lays her eggs in the stems of water plants.

Latin name	*Dytiscidae* (family)
Size	1/16–1 5/8 in (1.5–40 mm)
Habitat	Ponds, streams
Distribution	Worldwide

Latin name	*Scarabaeidae* (family)
Size	3/4–5 in (2–13 cm)
Habitat	Tropical forest
Distribution	Africa

Goliath beetle

The goliath beetle, found in Africa, is one of the largest and heaviest of all insects. Males are the giants; females are smaller and less brightly patterned. These beetles have strong front legs and are good climbers. They clamber up into trees in search of sap and soft fruit to eat. The heavily armored adults can fly, producing a sound similar to a small helicopter in flight.

Firefly

More than 2,000 species of firefly live in temperate and tropical environments around the world. Fireflies can produce a yellowish green light in a special area at the end of the abdomen. Each species of firefly flashes its light in a particular pattern to attract mates. Male fireflies have wings, but females are often wingless and look like larvae.

Latin name	*Lampyridae* (family)
Size	Up to ³/₈ in (1 cm)
Habitat	Temperate and tropical areas
Distribution	Worldwide

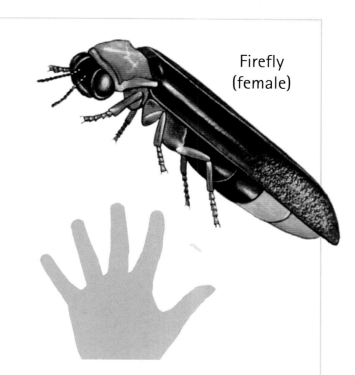

Firefly (female)

Click beetle

Click beetles make a clicking sound as they leap into the air to right themselves or avoid predators, giving these beetles their name. Some click beetles are colorful insects—some tropical species are brilliant metallic green—but most are dull brown or black in color. Their larvae, called wireworms, are pests that attack the roots of crops.

Latin name	*Dynastinae* (family)
Size	Up to 6 in (15 cm)
Habitat	Forest floor
Distribution	Tropical regions worldwide

Latin name	*Elateridae* (family)
Size	Up to 2½ in (6.5 cm)
Habitat	Vegetation
Distribution	Worldwide

Click beetle

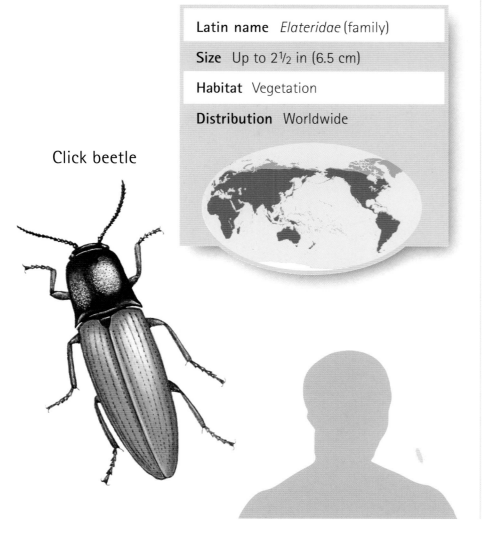

Rhinoceros beetle

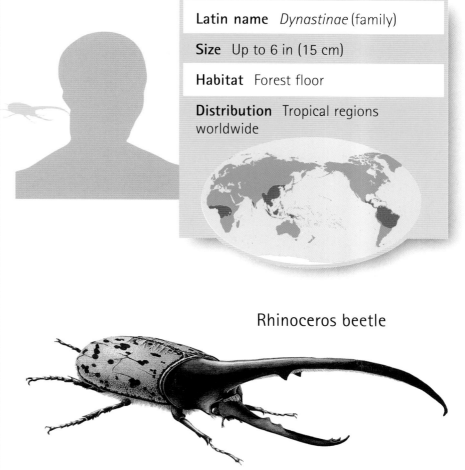

Rhinoceros beetle

The rhinoceros beetle is one of the largest beetles, the males possessing spectacular horns that give the beetle its name. Males use their horns to forage through heavy litter on the jungle floor, dig a burrow, and to battle against other males. Rhinoceros beetles are one of the strongest animals on the planet, in proportion to their size—they can lift up to 850 times their own weight.

Bees, wasps, ants, and termites

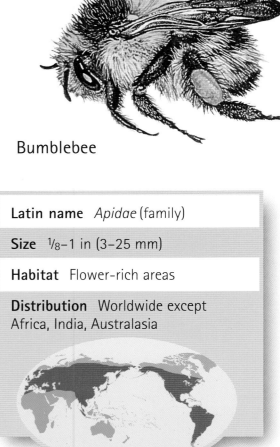
Bumblebee

Bees, wasps, and ants belong to a large group of insects known as the Hymenoptera. Many of these insects live in well-organized colonies containing thousands of individuals. Although bees, wasps, and ants vary greatly in appearance, most have a definite "waist" at the front of their abdomen. They have chewing mouthpieces and tonguelike structures for sucking nectar from flowers. Hymenopterans that do have wings have two pairs, but many worker ants are wingless. Termites have a similar social system, although they are not related to bees, wasps, and ants.

Latin name	*Apidae* (family)
Size	1/8–1 in (3–25 mm)
Habitat	Flower-rich areas
Distribution	Worldwide except Africa, India, Australasia

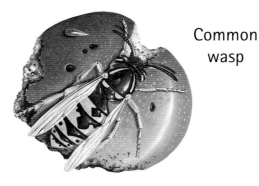
Common wasp

Common wasp

This insect typically is black and yellow in color. In spring, a single queen chooses a nest site, often in an abandoned mammal hole or a hollow tree, and lays her first eggs. The larvae hatch and become workers, foraging for food and maintaining the nest. A nest may house up to 10,000 wasps. Wasps feed on insects, nectar, and sweet fruit.

Latin name	*Vespula vulgaris*
Size	5/8–6/8 in (16–20 mm)
Habitat	Open land, forests
Distribution	Northern Hemisphere; introduced to Australia and New Zealand

Bumblebee

Bumblebees are usually black and yellow in color. In spring, the queen, which is the only bumblebee to live through the winter, collects pollen and nectar and makes food called beebread. Later, she lays eggs, and when the larvae hatch, they feed on the beebread. These larvae become adult worker bees and they take over the work of the colony.

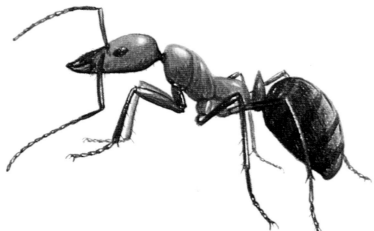

Red ant

Also called fire ants, red ants have copper-brown heads and bodies with darker abdomens. Colonies of red ants, founded by a single queen, build large mounds and feed on seeds, fruit, flowers, and sometimes small insects. Red ants often attack and kill small animals by biting them to get a grip and then injecting a toxin from their abdomens.

Latin name	*Formicidae* (family)
Size	²/₁₆–³/₁₆ in (3–5 mm)
Habitat	Moist areas
Distribution	Worldwide

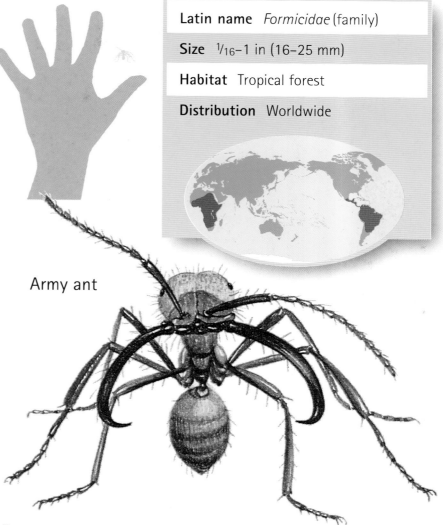

Army ant

Latin name	*Formicidae* (family)
Size	¹/₁₆–1 in (16–25 mm)
Habitat	Tropical forest
Distribution	Worldwide

Army ant

Unlike other ants, army ants do not build permanent nests. They march in search of prey, overpowering insects or other small creatures. They stop to produce eggs and remain in one place until the young have developed. The worker ants link their bodies together, making a temporary nest called a bivouac to protect the queen and young.

Subterranean termite

Subterranean termites are pest insects that live in colonies of up to a million individuals. They form networks of interconnected feeding sites beneath or above the soil surface. When subterranean termites search for food above ground, they may enter a house through small cracks or joints in the foundation, or by building shelter tubes along foundation walls.

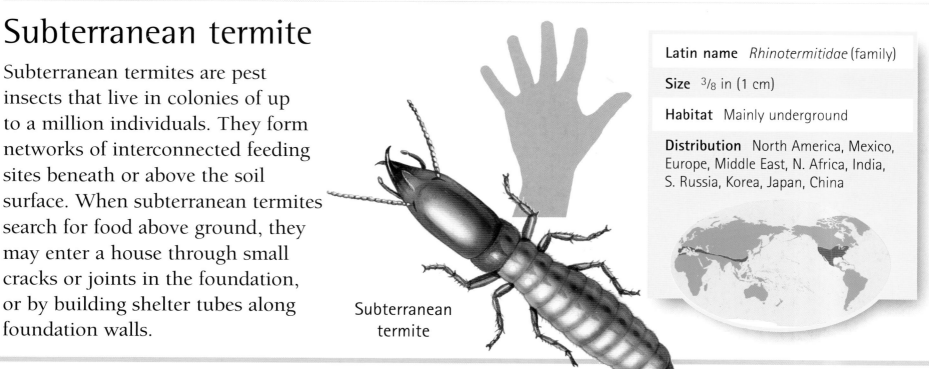

Subterranean termite

Latin name	*Rhinotermitidae* (family)
Size	³/₈ in (1 cm)
Habitat	Mainly underground
Distribution	North America, Mexico, Europe, Middle East, N. Africa, India, S. Russia, Korea, Japan, China

Social insects

While many hymenopterans lead solitary lives, ants and some bees and wasps live in complex social colonies. Typically, a colony is headed by a queen, which is the only female to mate and lay eggs. She is also larger than the other bees. Other females are workers who build the nest, gather food, and care for young but do not usually lay eggs. There are generally far fewer males in a colony. They do not work and are present only at certain times of the year to mate with new queens.

Above: Worker bees build nest cells from wax produced in glands on the underside of their abdomens.

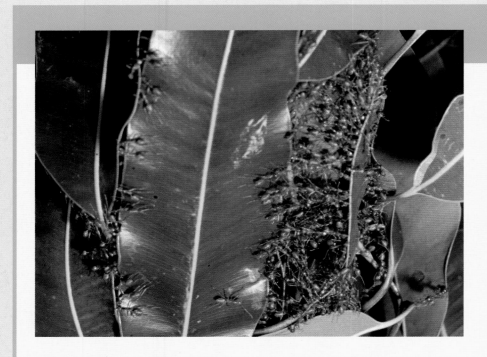

Green tree ants

Green tree ants are common in northern and central Queensland in Australia. They build large nests in trees by sticking the leaves at the end of branches together. Each colony has one queen and up to 500,000 workers, which patrol the tree nest and attack any invaders by biting them. A colony may span as many as 12 trees and contain as many as 150 nests.

Honeybees

Honeybees are the best known social bees. They make nests in hollow trees or in a hive provided by a beekeeper. The nest consists of sheets of hexagonal—six-sided—cells. These cells contain eggs and young as well as food stores of pollen and honey. Worker bees bring nectar and pollen back to the nest. When they return, the other bees collect the food stores.

Termites and leafcutter ants

Termites are small insects with biting mouthparts that live in huge colonies in nests made in wood, soil, or trees, or in specially built mounds. Unlike certain bees and ants, they lay their eggs in special chambers in the nest, not in individual cells. Some social insects, including leafcutter ants, grow their own food. They cut pieces of leaves and carry them back to their underground nest, where they are used to make compost heaps. The ants eat the special fungus that grows on the compost.

Leafcutter ant

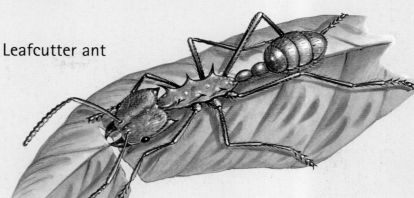

Above: Leafcutter ants use their cutting mouthparts to slice off pieces of leaves.

Termite mound

Right and below: Termite mounds may be more than 40 ft (12 m) tall.

Spiders

Spiders are arachnids, not insects. Arachnids generally have four pairs of legs but no wings or antennae. There are at least 35,000 known species of spiders in the world and many more yet to be named. All spiders can make silk using special glands at the end of the body, but not all build webs. Spiders use silk to line their burrows and some make silken traps that they hold between their legs to snare prey. Young spiders use long strands of silk as parachutes to fly away and find new territories. Many people are afraid of spiders, but only a few spiders have a venomous bite that is dangerous to humans. In fact, spiders do us a service by eating insects and keeping them under control.

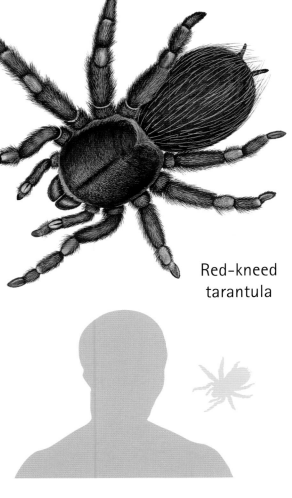

Red-kneed tarantula

Latin name	*Brachypelma smithi*
Size	Legspan: up to 6 in (15 cm)
Habitat	Deciduous forest, lowland scrub
Distribution	W. Mexico

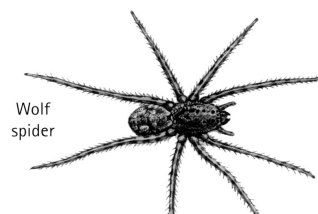

Wolf spider

Wolf spider

Fast-moving hunters like their namesake, wolf spiders creep up on prey and seize it after a final speedy dash. Most do not make webs. Wolf spiders have good eyesight, which helps them find prey. Their usually dull coloration helps them to blend into their habitat. The spider's bite is dangerous to humans, especially the young and elderly.

Latin name	*Lycosidae* (family)
Size	1/8–1 1/2 in (3–38 mm)
Habitat	Open lands, forests, woods
Distribution	Worldwide except Greenland and poles

Red-kneed tarantula

The red-kneed tarantula is a large spider with reddish orange markings on its legs. It hides inside its burrow during the day to avoid the sun and emerges at night to feed on crickets, grasshoppers, small snakes, frogs, spiders, and worms. The spider stuns prey using its two large, venomous fangs.

Spitting spider

The spitting spider is a pale yellow insect covered in varying sizes of black dots. It is an unusual hunter that approaches its victim, typically a small insect, and spits out two lines of a sticky substance from glands near its mouth. These fall in zigzags over the prey, pinning it down. The spider then kills its prey with a bite.

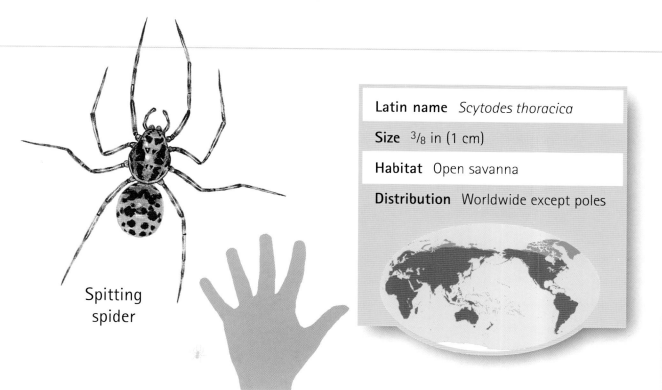

Spitting spider

Latin name	*Scytodes thoracica*
Size	³/₈ in (1 cm)
Habitat	Open savanna
Distribution	Worldwide except poles

Latin name	*Theridiidae* (family)
Size	Up to ¹/₂ in (1.3 cm)
Habitat	Urban and agricultural areas
Distribution	North America

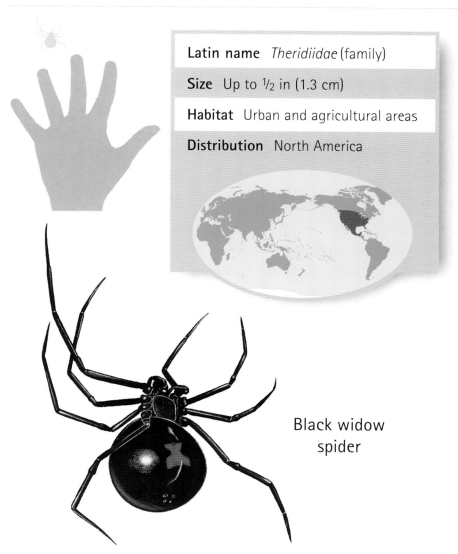

Black widow spider

Black widow spider

The three North American species of black widow spiders are best known for their dark coloration and red hourglass pattern. The female has comblike bristles on her back legs that she uses to throw strands of silk over prey that gets caught in her web. She also has a venomous bite, much more deadly than that of a rattlesnake. Males do not bite.

Crab spider

The crab spider moves by scuttling sideways like a crab. It typically lives on flowers, lying in wait with outstretched legs until a flying insect settles. It catches the insect by closing its powerful front legs, then bites it behind the head to kill it. The spider does not make webs, but the smaller males may use their silk to tie the females down before mating.

Latin name	*Thomisidae* (family)
Size	¹/₁₆–³/₈ in (1.6–10 mm)
Habitat	Flowers, vegetation
Distribution	Worldwide except Greenland and poles

Crab spider

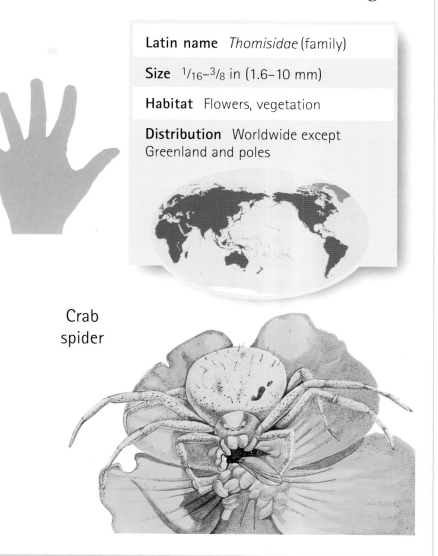

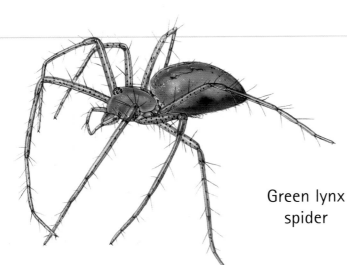

Green lynx
spider

Green lynx spider

The green lynx spider is a large, bright-green spider found on shrubs. It does not spin a web but chases its prey quickly from leaf to leaf. In fall, the female lays 25 to 600 orange eggs in each of four sacs. She hangs upside down from them and attacks any creatures that approach. The eggs hatch after about two weeks.

Latin name *Peucetia viridans*

Size 1/2–7/8 in (12–22 mm)

Habitat Shrubs, vegetation

Distribution S. U.S.A., Mexico, Central America, West Indies,

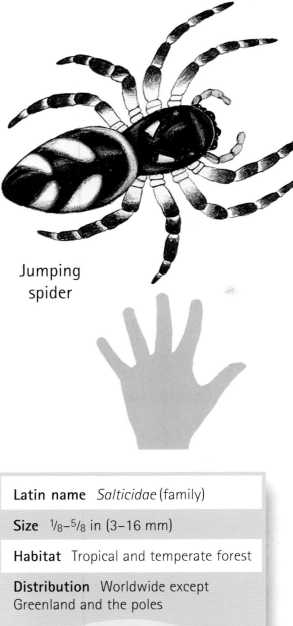

Jumping
spider

Latin name *Salticidae* (family)

Size 1/8–5/8 in (3–16 mm)

Habitat Tropical and temperate forest

Distribution Worldwide except Greenland and the poles

Common
house spider

Common house spider

Common house spiders build their tangled web in secluded locations, which can also house eggs contained in one or more spherical sacs. In appearance, these spiders are generally dull with brownish patterns. House spiders are harmless to humans and feed on household pests such as flies and mosquitoes.

Latin name *Achaearanea tepidariorum*

Size 1/4 in (6 mm)

Habitat Houses

Distribution North and South America; introduced worldwide

Jumping spider

Unlike most spiders, the jumping spider has good eyesight, which helps it find prey. Once it has spotted something, the spider leaps onto its victim. Before jumping, it attaches a silk thread to the ground as a safety line along which it can return to its hideout. They also use their silk to weave shelters for eggs. Jumping spiders can jump up to 30 times their body length.

Scorpions and mites

Scorpions, like spiders, are arachnids. There are many different kinds living everywhere from deserts to rainforests in warm parts of the world. They use a venomous sting at the end of the body to kill prey and to defend themselves. A few kinds of scorpion have venom so strong that it can kill a human, but the sting of most is no worse that that of a bee or wasp. Also in the arachnid group are tiny mites and ticks. Mites prey on other small insects. Ticks feed on the blood of birds, mammals, and reptiles.

Scorpion

The scorpion is a fierce hunter. It is armed with massive pincers for grasping its prey and a venomous stinger at the end of its body. Scorpions stay hidden during the day under stones or logs and come out at night to catch insects and spiders. They use their pincers to catch the prey, then either crush the prey or inject it with venom.

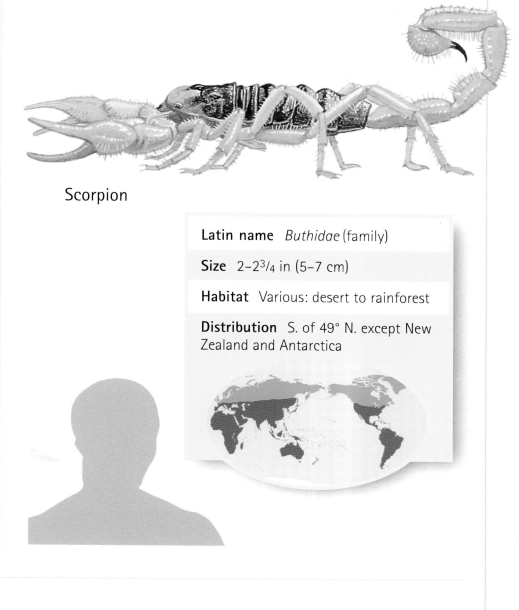

Scorpion

Latin name *Buthidae* (family)

Size 2–2³/₄ in (5–7 cm)

Habitat Various: desert to rainforest

Distribution S. of 49° N. except New Zealand and Antarctica

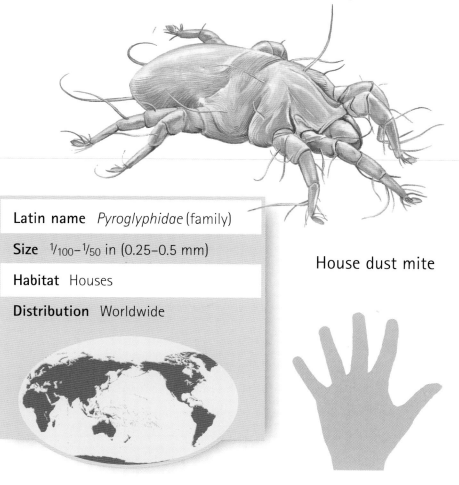

House dust mite

Latin name *Pyroglyphidae* (family)

Size ¹/₁₀₀–¹/₅₀ in (0.25–0.5 mm)

Habitat Houses

Distribution Worldwide

House dust mite

Dust mites thrive in mattresses, carpets, furniture, and bedding and are a common cause of asthma in humans. They live on tiny particles of organic matter. Some species prefer to eat skin cells, a large component of household dust; others prefer flour dust. Males live for 20 to 30 days, while a mated female dust mite can live for 10 weeks.

Glossary

amphibian A four-legged vertebrate that can live on land and in water and usually lays its eggs in water. Examples include frogs, toads, and salamanders.

anal fin The fin located behind the anus on the ventral (lower) surface of fish and certain marine mammals.

Arctic A region between the North Pole and the northern timberlines of North America, Europe, and Asia.

arthropod Invertebrate that has jointed limbs and a segmented body with an exoskeleton (a hard outer structure). Arthropods include insects, arachnids, and crustaceans. More than 80 percent of all known animal species are arthropods.

bill The horny part of the jaws of a bird; also known as a beak.

bird Any warm-blooded vertebrate with a body covered with feathers, forelimbs modified into wings, scaly legs, a beak, and no teeth, and bearing young in a hard-shelled egg.

camouflage Coloring or patterning that makes it difficult for enemies to see an animal against its background.

carnivore An animal that eats the flesh of other animals in order to survive; a meat-eating creature.

carrion The dead and rotting body of an animal.

caudal fin The tail fin on fish and certain marine mammals.

clutch A set of eggs produced or incubated at one time.

cold-blooded Used to describe an animal (such as a lizard or a snake) that cannot control its body temperature but must rely on the heat of the sun to keep it warm.

courtship In animals, the behavior that occurs before and during mating, often including elaborate displays.

crest A structure on top of the head, made of bone or feathers and skin. It is usually used by males in display to warn away other males and win a mate.

dorsal fin The main fin located on the back of fish and certain marine mammals.

evolution The process by which one species gives rise to another. Individual organisms pass on beneficial mutations (random changes in genes). As their kind multiplies, new species emerge.

extinct A species of animal that is no longer in existence. Dinosaurs are examples of extinct animals.

family A group of related genera, which are themselves groups of related species. The scientific name of a family usually ends in -idae.

gill The respiratory organ of aquatic animals, such as fishes, used to breathe the oxygen dissolved in water.

gland A cell, group of cells, or organ that produces a secretion in the body.

habitat The surroundings in which an animal lives, including the climate, water, and plant life.

herbivore An animal that eats plants.

incubation The act of keeping eggs warm by, for instance, sitting on them, so that the embryos inside develop.

insect Any animal of the class Insecta, which are small, air-breathing arthropods with bodies that are divided into three parts (head, thorax, and abdomen). They have three pairs of legs and usually two pairs of wings.

invertebrate An animal, such as an insect or mollusk, that lacks a backbone or spinal column.

iridescence Having lustrous, changing colors.

keel A structure, such as the breastbone of a bird, that resembles a ship's keel in function or shape, to which the flight muscles are attached.

larva The immature, wingless, feeding stage of an insect that undergoes complete metamorphosis.

mammal A four-legged vertebrate animal that has hair on its body and feeds its young on milk produced from its own body. Mammals include cats, horses, kangaroos, and humans.

mammary gland Any of the milk-producing glands in female mammals.

mangrove Any of several tropical evergreen trees or shrubs, which have stiltlike roots and stems and form dense thickets along tidal shores.

metamorphosis A marked change in form from one stage to the next in the life cycle of an organism, such as from the caterpillar to the pupa and from the pupa to the adult butterfly.

migration The periodic passage of groups of animals (especially birds or fishes) from one region to another for feeding or breeding.

mollusk An invertebrate with a soft, unsegmented body that is often enclosed in a shell. Snails, squids, and octopuses are all mollusks.

molt To periodically shed an outer covering, such as feathers or skin, that will be replaced by a new growth.

New World North America, Central America, and South America.

nymph The larval form of certain insects, such as grasshoppers, which usually resemble the adult form but are smaller and lack fully developed wings.

Old World Europe, Asia, and Africa.

omnivore An animal that feeds on both animals and plants. Human beings, pigs, and bears are examples of omnivores.

order A group of related families. Orders are divided into smaller groups, called suborders. Suborders are divided still further into infraorders, divisions, and families.

parasite An organism that lives on or in, and does harm to, an organism of another species, known as the host.

pectoral fin Either of a pair of fins usually situated behind the head of fish and some marine mammals, one on each side.

pelvic fin Either of a pair of fins on the lower surface of the body of fish or certain marine mammals, corresponding to the hind limbs of a land vertebrate.

plankton Small plant or animal organisms that float or drift in great numbers in fresh or salt water.

plumage The feather covering of birds.

pollen The powder inside a flower, which fertilizes other flowers.

predator An animal that hunts and kills other animals for food.

prey An animal hunted by a predator.

primate Any of various mammals of the order Primates, which have a highly developed brain, eyes facing forward, and opposable thumbs. Lemurs, apes, and humans are primates.

rain forest A tropical forest in an area of high annual rainfall.

ratite A member of a group of flightless birds with a flat breastbone.

reptile A vertebrate animal with scaly skin that lays eggs with tough, leathery shells. Dinosaurs, pterosaurs, and ichthyosaurs were all reptiles. Modern reptiles include tortoises, snakes, lizards, and crocodiles.

savanna Grassland region with scattered trees, usually in subtropical or tropical regions.

scavenger A creature that feeds on the remains of animals that have died naturally or been killed by other flesh-eaters.

spawn To deposit eggs directly into the water, as fish and amphibians do.

species In animals, a term for a group of animals that share very similar characteristics and can mate and produce young that can themselves have young.

Sternum A long, flat bone located in the center of the chest, serving as a support for the collarbone and ribs. It is also called a breastbone.

talon A claw, especially of a bird of prey.

temperate Not subject to prolonged extremes of hot or cold weather.

tropical Very hot and humid.

tundra Any of the vast, treeless plains of the Arctic regions of Europe, Asia, and North America.

tusk A long, pointed, or protruding tooth, usually one of a pair, as in the elephant, walrus, and wild boar.

vertebra One of the bones that make up a backbone. The backbone is made up of a number of vertebrae.

vertebrate An animal with a backbone. Mammals, birds, reptiles, amphibians, and fish are all vertebrates.

warm-blooded Describes an animal such as a mammal or bird that can control its own body temperature. Most reptiles and amphibians depend on the sun's heat to warm their bodies and are said to be cold-blooded.

wattle A fold of skin hanging down from the throat or chin of certain birds, such as the domestic chicken or turkey.

Index

Acknowledgments

Illustrators

Mammals Graham Allen, John Francis, Elizabeth Gray, Bernard Robinson, Eric Robson, Simon Turvey, Dick Twinney, Michael Woods

Birds Keith Brewer, Hilary Burn, Malcolm Ellis, Steve Kirk, Colin Newman, Denys Ovenden, Peter D. Scott, Ken Wood, Michael Woods

Reptiles and Amphibians John Francis, Elizabeth Gray, Steve Kirk, Alan Male, Colin Newman, Eric Robson, Peter D. Scott

Fish Robin Boutell, John Francis, Elizabeth Gray, Elizabeth Kay, Colin Newman, Guy Smith, Michael Woods

Insects and arachnids Robin Boutell, Joanne Cowne, Sandra Doyle, Bridget James, Steve Kirk, Adrian Lascombe, Alan Male, Colin Newman, Steve Roberts, Bernard Robinson, Roger Stewart, Colin Woolf

Photographic credits

All images supplied by Ecoscene except for:
122 Gregory Ochocki/Science Photo Library